Don't Run Out of MONEY

Don't Run Out of MONEY

How to Plan and Invest for Retirement Success

Sancus Press

*To my son, David Phillip, who always inspires me
to be my best.*

*To my mother, Phyllis, who left us way too soon.
I miss you every day.*

Table of Contents

Acknowledgments

Writing a book sounded like a good idea at the time. Little did I know how long of a journey it would be before it was complete. Along the way, the encouragement of many wonderful people got me through the many starts, stops, revisions, rewrites, and times I wanted to quit. Thank you to all of you who just listened. While it may not have seemed like much to you, it meant the world to me.

There are a special few I must mention separately. Without you, I would still just be talking about writing a book.

Jill Higgins - everything changed the day you came into my life. Your love and compassion inspire me beyond words. Thank you for all your help and motivation in the completion of this book.

Fred Chalmers - somehow thank you just isn't enough. I accomplish nothing without all your hard work and support. You are a huge part of everything that has happened and will happen. I am forever in your debt.

My son, David - you did your best to teach me how to be a writer. I hope I did you proud.

My father, Martin, the author and stepmother, Beverly, author and artist extraordinaire - your support, advice, and occasional life lessons are a big part of my life. Thank you for all you've done. Bev, thank you for an incredible cover design. Your talent as an artist never ceases to amaze me.

My brother, Ben - it has been a crazy journey through some very interesting times for both of us. The countless hours we spend sharing scotch, cigars, and conversation are more important to me than you'll ever know. Whether it was getting me through the tough times or just letting me ramble on about my ideas, you're always there for me.

Alicia Dunams and the team at Bestseller in a Weekend - without your help, this book would still just be a pile of paper. Thank you for teaching me how to get it done and helping me cross the finish line.

And, finally, to the families I serve in my practice, who every day place their trust in me to help them achieve their financial goals. Thank you.

Important Note To The Reader

As you will read in these pages, generic advice meant for the masses, if blindly followed, can be hazardous to your financial health. You and your situation are unique. As such, this book is not intended to give any specific tax or investment advice, nor does it suggest that the strategies discussed will be appropriate for your personal situation. It is vitally important that you seek the advice of knowledgeable financial professionals who can develop strategies and recommendations based on your personal situation and fully explain the benefits, risks, and alternatives. In addition, the strategies and techniques discussed exist as of the writing of this book. Changes in market conditions, tax laws, regulatory changes, or other unforeseen events may limit or eliminate their usefulness or availability in the future.

References to insurance product guarantees are subject to the claims-paying ability of the issuing insurance company; and, as always, past performance is no guarantee of future results.

Introduction

Ready or not, retirement is coming. For you, it might not be for a while, but it's coming. Will you be ready? Unfortunately, most people don't think they will. The number one concern of each generation, from the recently retired to the millennials, is running out of money in retirement. Many feel they'll never have enough money to retire.

It doesn't have to be that way. You probably have a picture in your mind of the retirement you want to live. This book will show you how to plan to make that a reality. Success doesn't happen by accident. You need to plan for it.

This book is a departure from what's usually written on the topic of retirement planning and personal finance in general. While most books ultimately attempt to steer you into a particular product or strategy, I have no such advice to offer. My goal is to bring a different perspective to this topic.

Unlike many in this industry who have spent their entire careers selling stuff, I bring over 30 years of financial markets and corporate finance experience to the party. During this time, I have managed the financial risk, as well as diverse financial duties and responsibilities, for major corporations and started and ran a few of my own companies. I have worked with most of the major commercial banks and Wall Street firms, managed a large pension fund, designed global currency hedging strategies, worked on teams that took a company public, and set up joint ventures in China, just to name a few. I have held executive financial positions, including that of a Corporate Treasurer and Chief Financial Officer of the International Division of a major consumer products company.

Today, I help the families I serve plan for their financial success.

My financial background allows me to approach retirement planning from a unique perspective. I understand how the financial game is played. Instead of filling these pages with market speak and financial jargon and buzzwords, I will take a simple, jargon-free, and common-sense approach to explain and replace the misinformation about the markets, finance, planning, and the players and products that we blindly accept with the facts necessary to make better financial decisions. What you'll discover in these pages is presented with a single goal in mind; to refocus the reader's attention away from the noise of the media, the markets, the Internet, and the financial gurus, and back to where it needs to be: on achieving your financial goals.

Throughout this book, I will challenge some of the long-held beliefs you may have about the markets, investing, retirement planning, and many other financial topics. I will show how much of what you accept as fact is not.

One of the keys to financial success is the creation of a financial plan, a roadmap to your financial future. You will learn the difference between a financial plan that will help you achieve your goals and one that's only purpose is to sell you a financial product. I will teach you the framework that I use with the families I work with to help them achieve their financial goals.

Be advised that this book won't unveil a get-rich- quick scheme or some mystical system that will make your retirement dreams come true. There's nothing for sale here. I won't show you how putting your hard-earned money into one magic financial product will solve all your problems. That's part of the reason we're in this mess. This is a challenge—a challenge to change the way you approach your finances and your retirement planning.

If you're the do-it-yourselfer searching for the Holy Grail, the guru seeker looking for easy answers, or one that thinks the government will or should provide for all our needs, this isn't the place for you. If, on the other hand, you're willing to commit some time and a little effort to help secure your future, then read on - you've come to the right place.

Retirement is a long journey. Like any journey, proper planning is needed to ensure success. It's all about being able to answer two questions:

- Will you have enough money to last throughout your retirement?
- Will you be living the retirement you imagine?

Failure cannot be an option. Let me help put you on the path to success.

Before we begin, there's one more thing: There's been a lot written lately about the death of the American Dream. That's sad. After all, when did "Ask not what your country can do for you..." become "I want my free stuff?" The road to financial well-being and security might not be easy. It will be paved with hard work, discipline, and perhaps even a little sacrifice.

Contrary to what some of our political leaders and commentators would like us to believe, the American Dream is not dead. It cannot be killed, nor can it be stolen from us. It cannot be taken from us by those more successful, nor can it simply be given to us by political will. The American Dream is alive and well, just where it's always been, safely hidden away for those willing to act to achieve their dreams.

Your American Dream is waiting. Let's go get it!

PART I

Question Everything

CHAPTER 1

There's a Bad Moon Rising

It's hard to turn on the news without hearing a story about the looming retirement crisis in America. It's well chronicled that 10,000 baby boomers are turning 65 each day. The future and survival of Social Security is a never-ending political debate, and the cost of healthcare seems to be increasing at exponential rates at the same time that we're living longer lives. Who would have thought, as many news outlets report, that living longer would be cause for a crisis? Also, many people have suffered devastating financial setbacks due to bad financial decisions or the aftermath of the financial crisis of 2008. These stories almost always conclude that we're headed toward a financial crisis unlike any in history.

It's easy to look around and see that there may be a crisis out there. Walk into a supermarket or fast food restaurant and see who is ringing up your order or bagging your groceries. Some years ago, it was a high school kid making a few bucks after school. Now it's likely to be a retiree who went back to work to supplement their income or qualify for health insurance. Seniors who, for whatever reason, didn't save enough during their best earning years are desperately looking for work in greater numbers. Few companies are interested in hiring them, and it only gets worse as they reach 70 or 80.

Many people, who expected to retire at 65 or 67, find they must keep working to survive, pay their bills, avoid bankruptcies and foreclosures, or continue to live respectable lives. They can't survive on Social Security alone, and they have little else to sustain them unless they can continue to earn regular paychecks. How long can they continue to work until age and frailty catch up to them?

In economic and financial terms, many are experiencing a retirement crisis. Hopefully, you'll never be part of it, but it does affect entire segments of our society - college graduates and those who never went to college, men and women, especially single women. Caucasians and minorities, people with long work histories who have always lived paycheck to paycheck but have never been able to save. The median family of retirement age has only $12,000 in savings[1]. That just won't cut it.

Is There a Crisis?

There are certainly those who are struggling and those who are not prepared for retirement. There are also those who have been dealt a financial blow from a job loss, health issues, or some other event that was outside of their control. Unfortunately, this has and always will be the case for a segment of the population. Then there are those who continually fall for the latest can't-miss investments, leverage their futures by accumulating large amounts of debt, and play keep-up-with-the-Jones' with every aspect of their lives. For those who have fallen into this trap, there certainly is a crisis for which there are no easy answers. But what about the rest of us?

While it may be tempting to draw conclusions about a retirement crisis based on media reports, you must be careful before concluding that it will affect you. What is noticeably missing from these stories are solutions.

Many of the reports draw their conclusions from the reporter's analysis of the results of the plethora of surveys that attempt to connect the public's confidence in their ability to retire at some point with their actual ability to retire. These surveys often report that a high percentage of Americans have a low level of confidence in their ability to be ready for retirement.

Confidence numbers are a misleading and potentially dangerous measure of anything financial or economic. In most cases, a person's confidence level, in financial terms, is nothing more than a direct reflection of the current state of the economy, politics, or the stock market. When things are perceived to be good, confidence is high. When perceptions are that things are bad, confidence is low. Often, the only difference between the two is the reporting on the news. Have you ever come across someone who gets depressed when the market is in the toilet, even though they have nothing invested in the market?

True confidence in one's ability to retire can be gained by planning and doing what's necessary to prepare for the retirement they desire. It has nothing to do with the state of the stock market or economy or how you feel about the current situation in Washington.

Also, these reports spend most of their time talking about the average person, the average investor, or the average retiree. This is useless for you. As I will state often throughout this book, you are not average. How you compare to the average is meaningless. Are YOU preparing for retirement? Are YOU saving enough? Do YOU have a plan? Just by reading this book you're already above average. You're starting the process. There's a long list of questions you need to answer throughout this process. The common denominator to all of them is YOU - not some average.

The Rules of Retirement Have Changed

If there truly is a crisis on the horizon, it exists not solely because of demographics, government policies, bad decisions, or bad luck but because the rules for retirement have changed dramatically from those of just a few decades ago. The solution to averting a crisis lies in understanding and adapting to these changes. A solution will require you to rethink your approach to retirement and your long-held beliefs about the market. The adages, conventional wisdom, and rules of thumb you accept as truth and blindly follow must be analyzed to determine if they are financial laws or just outdated market myths. You must take a hard look at the approach and methods that have become commonplace for managing your money to see if they are appropriate for achieving your financial goals. The financial landscape has changed and so must your approach to planning and investing.

Planning for retirement is getting a lot tougher. It wasn't always that way. Once upon a time, retirement was a lot easier. For many of our parents and grandparents, a gold watch and a generous pension were the rewards for a lifetime of service to a company. When they combined their pension with Social Security, some savings, a house that was paid for, and most important, no debt, most could live out their golden years with some sense of financial security. Sadly, those days are all but gone. What happened?

Death of the Pension

Major changes have occurred in the investment world since we entered the 2000s that have dramatically impacted the way we approach retirement planning. One of these changes was the further decline of companies offering the classic defined-benefit pension plan, a continuation of a trend that had begun years before.

When stock prices surged during the late 1990s, the rise in investment values caused many pension plans to be considered overfunded by IRS guidelines. Many companies (in addition to many state and local governments) took advantage of this and either discontinued funding their pensions or removed funds from the plans altogether (this was the case with many state and local governments.) When the music stopped and the stock market and interest rates plummeted, many firms, especially in weaker industries, went bankrupt.

This was partially due to their inability to meet their now much higher pension obligations. As a result, many surviving firms have re-evaluated their retirement plans. To reduce risk and liability for the company, they have discontinued their pension plans altogether, choosing to replace them with defined-contribution plans such as the 401(k). Since 2000, the number of firms continuing to offer defined-benefit pension plans has steadily dwindled. Today, less than 20 percent of Fortune 500 companies still offer these plans to their employees, down from almost 60 percent in 1998[2].

The transition from defined-benefit to defined- contribution plans has had a profound impact on an employee's ability to prepare for retirement primarily because **defined-contribution plans, as designed, were never intended to be a replacement for a pension.**

The 401(k) and similar defined-contribution plans were conceived and enacted in the 1980s as a way for employees to supplement their retirement savings by making contributions to the plans with pretax money. Tax deferral was appealing to many due to the relatively high-income tax rates at the time. Deferring the income tax until retirement would theoretically subject the income to a lower tax rate in the future than would currently be paid. Also, many employers matched a percentage of the employee's contributions, making plans more appealing.

While the 401(k) was and is a tremendous benefit for those who could participate, when conceived and designed, it was never intended to be a replacement for a pension. This is where the real crisis begins.

The Investing Goal Has Changed

Defined-benefit pensions were designed and professionally managed to provide the retiree with a guaranteed income for the balance of their life, usually with the option to continue benefits in some amount for the life of their spouse. If you asked a holder of a pension the value of their benefit, the answer would be the amount of monthly income they will receive or the percentage of their current salary. Social Security is thought of in the same manner. The goal of these instruments is to provide income that is guaranteed and can never run out.

The investment decisions for the pension plans were placed in the hands of professional investment managers usually overseen by a pension committee inside the company. The goal of the management was to obtain a return sufficient to fund the liabilities of the plan—not for the maximum rate of return. As such, these plans are invested in portfolios that are generally moderate on the risk scale.

The move away from the defined-benefit pension to defined-contribution plans has transferred the risk from the company directly to the employee. Investment decisions that were once made by professionals and overseen by committees are now the responsibility of each employee.

Do you remember when you were first eligible to contribute to your 401(k)? If the story goes like many I've seen or heard, you received a packet from Human Resources, filled out a bunch of forms, then you got to the part where it asked how you would like to invest your money. Chances are, your job and educational background have nothing to do with finance or investing. What did you do? As the story usually goes, you asked the person in the next cubicle for advice. After all, they've been in the 401(k) for six months; they must know what's best! Subsequent investment decisions are made the same way, if any decisions are made at all. Does this sound like any way to manage what one day will need to become your largest asset?

Technology and Investment Knowledge

Today, we live in an incredible time. The technological explosion of the past 20 or so years has given us access to information at our fingertips that just a short time ago was reserved for only those who were willing to spend significant time, effort, or money to obtain. We are now connected to everyone and every bit of information by simply reaching into our pockets for our smartphones. We can now find out just about everything, about anything, from anywhere, at any time. Just like TV's space-age family, the Jetsons, these technological advances bring with them the hope of simpler lives where we can accomplish more, in less time, with less effort.

Even with all this new technology, or maybe because of it, today's world is getting more complex. The world of finance and particularly our personal finances is certainly no exception. The technology boom, the Internet, and the explosion of financial media have given us the promise of easy access to all the information we think we need to be successful with our finances on our own. And there's the real problem.

Many financial firms spend vast amounts of advertising dollars to convince us that playing the market is the key to a sound retirement. Regardless of your background, financial knowledge, or ability, they entice you with free trades, tools, and strategies that, according to the commercials, can make anyone, even a baby, a successful trader or investor. Celebrities show us how it's possible to trade stocks from anywhere - anytime we get an idea. Even after many suffer devastating loses, they keep coming back for more. They make it seem so easy.

This market-centric attitude has changed the way retirement funds are managed. Instead of focusing on creating future income, investment decisions are now focused on account balances, rates of return, volatility, and whatever measure the financial media would have us believe is important this week. While this strategy is fine if your goal is to make money for the financial firms, it has its problems if your primary concern is creating a level of future income so you can live the retirement you desire.

This stuff is not as simple as some would like you to think, and Americans, for the most part, are not as smart as they think they are. Despite having free and easy access to a seemingly unlimited amount of information, Americans rank 14th in the world in financial literacy[3].

In a 2017 study conducted by the American College of Financial Services, Americans between the ages of 60 and 75 were asked a variety of financial and attitudinal questions. Roughly 75 percent of the respondents failed the 38-question quiz, and only 6 percent could score an A or B. Despite the poor performance, 61 percent of the respondents stated they were highly knowledgeable about retirement planning[4].

In a similar study, this time covering millennials and conducted by George Washington University, only 8 percent of those polled had what the researchers considered a high-level of knowledge about personal finance. Once again, despite the performance, 70 percent of those who took part in the study believed their financial knowledge was at a high-level[5].

The retirement crisis exists not solely because of demographics, government policies, bad decisions, or bad luck but because the average person just doesn't have the financial knowledge necessary to be successful. **Putting complex investment decisions in the hands of individuals who do not have the knowledge or skills to make them is a bad idea and one worthy of creating a crisis.**

Have You Lost Your Focus?

Somewhere along the way, we took our eye off the ball. We lost our focus. The market-centric approach has not only changed the way we manage our savings but has, more importantly, made us forget what's important. After all, what's the point of all the effort put into saving and investing our hard-earned money? Why not just spend it - live for today? Is it for no other reason than to make more money with no specific result? Has beating the market really become the financial goal for our lives? Or do we have some other reason, some goal in mind, that makes us put our money at risk? Is our 401(k), IRA, or brokerage account balance the ends or simply the means that will enable us to achieve our goals?

I'm guessing that if you're taking the time to read this book, you've started to give some thought to your retirement. That can be scary. Where do you start? If you're like most, you probably have some idea of how you imagine your ideal retirement. You have some plan in your head. You have some idea of the result you want from of all those years spent working. You have some vision of what success may look like.

How do you define success, and how do you get there? How do you turn that idea, that thought, into an action? That, my friend, is the key.

If you turn on the TV, it seems that everyone knows what success means. The financial companies, gurus, and so-called experts spend millions of dollars to get you to buy into their idea of success, which usually includes images of sailboats, fast cars, and exotic locales. They then try to convince you to exchange your dollars for their solution. Does this make sense to you? How can someone help you if they have no idea of what they're helping you to do? Are you interested in someone else's idea of success?

Success is personal, individual, and unique to you. You'll hear that quite a bit throughout these pages. The only person who can define your success is you.

To avert a potential crisis in your retirement, a change in thinking may be required. It's not about Wall Street and your portfolio - it's about you and what's happening on Your Street, in your home, and at your kitchen table. Your success will come not from some magical financial product, but from careful and detailed planning to ensure that you'll be able to do the things that will make your retirement worth living.

You must dispense with the short-term, beat-the- market thinking that has done nothing more than generate miserable returns for most investors. Your focus needs to shift from the markets to YOU. Only then can you gain the patience and vision required for long-term financial success. This is all about you and achieving your goals.

Is there a retirement crisis on the horizon? Are we already in one? Perhaps the better question is, are YOU heading for a crisis? Unfortunately for some, bad luck, bad decisions, or bad planning has already turned their retirement dreams into a nightmare. For the rest of us, there may still be time.

CHAPTER 2

If You Fail to Plan

When it comes to retirement, each of us has a different idea of what the ideal retirement will be. Is yours to bask in luxury on a quiet beach, cocktail in hand and not a care in the world? Would you buy a boat and sail to some exotic location? Maybe your desire is to move to a climate where your hardest decision was whether to play golf or tennis, beach or pool. Or, maybe your goals are simpler—a desire to turn a hobby into a small business, volunteer, or just spend time with the family and look after the grandkids. Whatever your goals for retirement may be, you'll need a plan for getting there. Dreams do not just magically happen.

One of the most heralded writers of all time, Edgar Allen Poe, wrote his classic books in a consistent pattern. He wrote the ending first, then went back and worked from the beginning, making sure that every element of his book was a step toward the end he had envisioned.

Hall of Fame basketball coach, Red Holtzman, was once asked about his long run of success in the New York Knickerbockers' glory years. He replied, "I always plan for the worst, then I pray for the best."

What do these two scenarios have in common? They are commitments to planning. The importance of planning cannot be overemphasized.

The Importance of Planning

In business, a solid and concise business plan has always been looked upon as one of the requirements for success. Seldom can a start-up wing it and survive to make a profit. In sports, after a big win for your favorite football team, you will almost always hear the head coach credit the team's success on their commitment to, and execution of, their game plan. Success in almost any endeavor is usually the direct result of following a plan.

Your personal life is no different. How much easier is your trip to the grocery store when you've done some advance planning and created a list? There's seldom a need to go back to the store because you forgot something important, like the coffee you just ran out of this morning or tonight's dinner. What about your vacation? Maybe being spontaneous and just taking off works when you're young and without a family, but the results could be a disaster when there are kids involved.

The need for planning increases as the cost of failure increases. Forgetting the coffee at the store is an inconvenience. Running out of money in retirement is a disaster.

While it is possible to be successful without a plan, often that can be attributed to luck. Going back to your favorite football team, not executing a plan, or worse yet, not having a plan, is a sure-fire way to be defeated. Even the best, most talented teams will have a hard time if they don't construct and execute a plan. This is also certainly the case with your finances. Having a large account balance is no guarantee of success. Just ask Bob and Joan.

The Sad Saga of Bob and Joan

I have no better way to illustrate the importance of financial planning than to tell the story of Bob and Joan. A few years ago, I received a call from Bob (not his real name.) He and his wife, Joan (not her real name either), had just sold their house and moved into a retirement community. The proceeds of the sale of the house were pretty much all the cash they had left, and they had no idea what they should do.

Bob had retired back in 1999. He sold a car dealership for an amount that should have been sufficient to fund their retirement. Up to this point, Bob and Joan lived a very comfortable life. They were never left wanting and took great pride in being able to help their kids and grandkids in any way they could. Their greatest joy was spoiling their grandchildren by buying them anything they wanted. They traveled often and when not traveling were seldom found just sitting at home. This was a lifestyle they wanted to continue as long as they were physically able. They sacrificed in the past. They did not want to sacrifice now.

Not knowing much about investing or financial planning, when Bob sold his business, he turned to a local financial advisor, Jim, whose office was down the street from Bob's car dealership. Bob had known Jim casually through his involvement with the local Chamber of Commerce and felt comfortable working with him. Bob asked Jim to take care of his money. As Bob told it, their discussion revolved around investments, risk, and how long he wanted the money to last. Bob's answer to that question would lead to the sale of the house all those years later and our meeting that day.

As Bob told it, his answer to that question was "make my money last until I'm 85. I'll be dead by then." Unfortunately, Joan was not there when this conversation took place. She trusted her husband, and his financial decisions to that point had mostly been good. After all, they had a pretty good life. Until now.

If you're paying attention, you can probably spot a few of the problems. Jim had done exactly what Bob had asked him to do. You see, the day I met Bob and Joan was one week after Bob's 85th birthday, and the money was gone. The problem was Bob was not dead! To compound the problem, Joan was ten years younger than Bob.

Bob and Joan now had to face the stark reality that life was going to change. They had been spending at a rate that they could not sustain because no one told them otherwise. Their unsustainable lifestyle, along with the market implosions due to the dot-com bust of the early 2000's and the financial crisis of 2008, had left Bob and Joan broke, and they never saw it coming. Even after selling their house, the cost of the upscale retirement community was unsustainable. At their current spending rate, the proceeds of the house sale would last for only a few years.

Bob and Joan could not accept the fact that they would have to make another move, this time to a much more modest community. Also, they would have to drastically downgrade their lifestyle. There was nothing I could do. There was no advice, no magic financial product that would allow them to live out their retirement in the lifestyle they had become accustomed to for all these years.

How could this happen? Now, to be fair, I was not there for the initial conversations between Bob and Jim. However, during my conversations with Bob, it became apparent there was a misunderstanding between what Bob thought Jim was doing and Jim's actual role. You see, even though Jim referred to himself as a financial advisor, he was a stockbroker or registered representative. Where Bob was under the impression that Jim was looking out for all his financial matters, all he was concerned with was watching his investments.

Bob, as is too often the case, thought his account statement was his financial plan. Bob and Joan's lack of a true, comprehensive financial plan allowed the unthinkable to happen. They ran out of money. Bob's misunderstanding of the importance of a true financial plan had a devastating effect on his family.

American families need, want, and benefit from comprehensive financial planning and advice. Bob and Joan's story is an example of the problems that occur when a family has no financial plan. I do not doubt that if Bob and Joan had realized the dangers they faced from their lack of planning, they would have never been in this situation.

What is Financial Planning?

Before we can get into the nuts and bolts of creating your financial plan, you must understand what financial planning is and, more important, what it is not.

What is financial planning? Well, depending on who you ask, you will get many different answers. This may come as a surprise to you—it shocked me—but there is no generally accepted or regulatory definition of financial planning or financial advice. Definitions will vary from advisor to advisor and firm to firm. The financial planning and advice that you receive will be defined by the advisor you're speaking with and the products he is selling.

The American College, one of the preeminent institutions for the education of financial advisors, recognizes the lack of clarity about the exact nature of financial planning as a concern.

> One factor that has hampered the development of financial planning as a discipline and as a profession is the fact that there has been very little agreement among advisors as to exactly what financial planning is. Indeed, there are as many definitions of financial planning as there are people who believe they are engaged in it[6].

Perhaps from the perspective of the American College and other financial planning organizations, the vagueness over the definition of financial advice is appropriate. According to their text, if an advisor is following the planning framework they teach, it does not matter if the advisor sells or advises in only one or more narrow areas, they can still be considered practicing financial planning[7]. That's a pretty convenient determination for the advisors and should be a concern for you.

It seems a bit optimistic, if not ridiculous, to think that an advisor will spend the time to do a complete and unbiased (from a product perspective) financial analysis if they only have one product they can or must sell. It seems more likely any analysis will be part of a selling system designed to get you to buy their solution. All too often that's exactly how it works—and that's a problem.

Also, if you listen to the financial media or believe the countless commercials you're subject to from the brokerage and financial services industry, you might think that a financial plan is simply the financial products and investments you own or that they want to sell you. Nothing could be further from the truth. Unfortunately, misconceptions and misrepresentations concerning the financial planning process have left many individuals believing they have a financial plan when they don't.

I see this problem almost every time I do a presentation or meet with a prospective family for the first time. I always ask if they've done any financial planning and if they have a financial plan. This is of importance if they are currently working with a financial professional of some type. In almost every instance where the prospect tells me that they have a financial plan, when they give me what they consider to be their plan to review, it's no more than a brokerage account statement or the statement of some other financial product. **A portfolio or financial product is not a financial plan.**

If you went to a stockbroker, gave him your hard- earned money, and all he did was invest it, you have a portfolio. You do not have a financial plan. Likewise, if you were advised by an insurance agent to purchase a cash value life insurance policy or an annuity, you have a financial product, not a financial plan. That is not to say that these products and portfolios are necessarily bad. In many cases, quite the contrary. They are just not a financial plan.

Financial products and investment vehicles are necessary, but they are not your financial plan. They are simply some of the tools that will be used to execute your plan and enable you to reach your goals. If the discussions with your financial advisor are strictly about where to put your money, you need to find a new advisor. Could this type of misrepresentation be part of the reason for the level of mistrust of financial professionals?

So, what is financial planning? It's much more than a ballpark guesstimate of what your portfolio will be worth at some point in the future. While, as I will show, financial planning can take many forms, the process must take a detailed look at your current and future financial picture—the result being a roadmap to help solve your problems and answer the questions that concern you, while optimizing your financial assets to achieve your financial goals. Hang in there. I'll get into much greater detail later.

What's in a Name?

Financial planning may go by many different names depending on who you are meeting with and, unfortunately, what they may be trying to sell you. Retirement Planning, Retirement Income Planning, Investment Planning or Consulting, Insurance Planning, Estate Planning, College Planning, the list can be endless but, in most cases, covers just a narrow swath of your financial life.

I have a different view on the subject. Comprehensive Financial Planning needs to encompass every aspect of your financial life because each issue is intertwined with every other issue. For example, each time you decide to invest a dollar, say in your IRA, you are deciding not to invest that same dollar someplace else. Instead of the IRA, would you be better off putting that dollar into an insurance plan or a brokerage account, paying off your credit card, or maybe just keeping it liquid? Only by analyzing all the interconnected parts of your financial situation can a financial plan be developed, and recommendations be made, that will help you reach your goals. How can an advisor who provides advice in only one of these areas provide the same plan? It is more likely that these narrow recommendations will be geared toward a product sale that could be potentially unsuitable for your needs.

Within the realm of comprehensive financial planning, there are different methods and approaches that a financial advisor can take to complete the planning process. I would not be so arrogant as to assume that the process and methods I will disclose in this book are the best or only method available. The importance here is that you gain the knowledge to identify the difference between true comprehensive financial advice and the professionals that provide it, from the practitioners of narrow, sales-based advice geared toward doing nothing more than selling you something. The financial world may consider them both financial advice, but I don't, and neither should you.

The Journey of a Lifetime

You have one life. Your financial plan needs to cover every aspect of your financial life from today until the end. That could be a long time. We are living longer, and that's a good thing. That is, unless you haven't planned on living as long as you may. According to the Society of Actuaries 2014 Mortality Tables, for healthy upper-middle-class couples aged 65 today, there's a 43 percent chance that one or both will live to age 95. By 2029, the odds climb to 50 percent[8]. That means that if you make it to retirement age, you have a very good chance of living well into your nineties.

Life expectancy had risen steadily since the turn of the century as medical knowledge and technology have increased. What will happen to those statistics as medicine progresses further and comes ever closer to a cure for some of the biggest killers, such as cancer and heart disease? This good news can quickly turn into a nightmare if you aren't prepared for the possibility of extended life.

Financial planning needs to be done for the long term, not just for your most recent issue. Think about it for a minute. If you start doing serious planning at the age of 40, given how long you may live, your financial plan needs to work for at least the next 40 or 50 years, or more. Wouldn't it be nice to have a financial plan that can take you that far and beyond? Are you starting to see why you need to change your focus to the long term?

The Art of Planning

So far, I've written a lot about the need for planning. I hope by now you get the message. But what is the outcome of all this planning? What will you have when you're done?

The goal of comprehensive financial planning is to give you a roadmap from where you are today to achieving your life's goals, whatever they may be. For some, it may include the answers to the issues that are keeping them up at night. How can you pay down debt or afford college for your children? For others, it may include how you can afford the beach house you want. Everyone will want to know when and how they'll be able to retire. The outcome of the planning process will be different for each family simply because each family has different goals, issues, and needs.

Your comprehensive financial plan needs to be a concise, working document that is reviewed and updated at least annually. It is not a static document that's out of date the minute it's completed. You may have one of those sitting on your shelf collecting dust right now. Your plan should be able to be easily updated as your goals change to see how those changes will affect you in the long term.

For example, let's assume that you and your spouse just completed your financial planning. Your plan was put in place and has you on-track to retire at 65. So far, so good. A few months later, you decide you want to make a major change.

In addition to the many goals you have, you now want to include some pretty extensive travel starting right away and continuing into retirement. The question is, what impact would the travel have on your retirement plan.

Having a comprehensive financial planning framework in place should allow your advisor to easily determine the impact of this change and whether other changes will need to be made.

Perhaps this exercise shows that while it may be possible to retire at 65, it would be tight. Things would have to fall just right, and there couldn't be any surprises, or you might have to cut back on your travel plans. That's something you don't want to do.

Let's assume for a moment that your advisor reviewed their findings with you and showed you that if you worked until age 67, just two additional years, the success of your plan would be almost a certainty. Realizing ten years before retirement that you may need to work two extra years is certainly better than getting to 65 and finding out you don't have the money to retire and would have to continue working or significantly change your spending plans. This is the reason we plan—to answer questions and eliminate surprises.

There are No Easy Answers

A word of caution. Planning for your future will take some work. It should. It's important. Except for your health and the health of your loved ones, is there a more important topic or bigger worry than that of your financial security?

Unfortunately, many individuals - and advisors - either can't, won't, or don't know how to do the work necessary to create a comprehensive financial plan. Instead, they rely on quick answers they can obtain from throwing a few numbers into an online calculator and combining the answer with some outdated rules-of-thumb to produce their Plan. While this may be a great sales tactic, these shortcuts can never hope to produce accurate results. Instead, they will most likely produce results that are much better or much worse than reality.

Both are bad answers. I hate rules-of- thumb and shortcuts in general that are used by those too lazy or unskilled to do the real work. I'll get into a further discussion and analysis of these shortcuts later. But for now, don't you need - and deserve - better?

Completing comprehensive financial planning will answer the questions that you have - even if you're afraid to ask. It will reduce or eliminate the impact of the inevitable surprises that occur all the time. Knowing your current and projected financial situation gives you the ability to make decisions and enact changes when you still have time and earnings to do something. If there are problems, you can correct them before it's too late. Once retired, it becomes very difficult, if not impossible, to correct deficiencies. At that point, you may be stuck in a retirement situation that's less than what you imagined. Planning may not be the sexy topic that investments are, but it's the first and most important step in achieving your goals.

Setting Your Goals

I hope by now you see the importance and the need for comprehensive financial planning - your roadmap to achieving financial success. It may seem a bit overwhelming. Where do you start?

The foundation on which your financial plan will be built and the yardstick by which your success will be measured is the establishment and definition of your goals. Think about that for a minute. How can you create a plan for your future if you don't include all the things that you need, want, and desire? Isn't that the point of retirement?

Think about it this way. Your goals are your destination. Don't they deserve a little effort, or will you leave it to luck?

All too often, this is where the problems begin. We are notoriously poor at setting goals. For some reason, people spend about as much time thinking about and defining their goals as they do ordering from the drive-up window at their favorite fast food joint. You know how that goes. You pull into the drive-up, hope there's at least a car or two ahead of you, so you have time to think. Suddenly, you hear those words, "May I help you?" and you're on the clock. The pressure builds; there are cars behind you. You blurt out whatever comes to mind and instantly have regrets and remorse. Too late. Hope you enjoy the McRib.

How much better would the process be if you had your order thought out and written down beforehand and the only thing you needed to do was read it?

Every book and article I've ever read about success teaches that one characteristic of highly successful individuals is that they write down their goals and review them often. Many start each day by reviewing the piece of paper containing their goals. I'm amazed how often I sit down with a couple and find out that they have never discussed their goals with each other. This leads to some pretty interesting and sometimes emotional conversations. If you plan on taking this long journey with someone, wouldn't it be nice to plan on ending up in the same place?

The One Must-Have Goal

When I start the planning process with a new family, we spend a great deal of time establishing their goals - the must have and the nice to have. At some point in the process, I explain to them that there is one goal I have for them—a goal that is so important for them to adopt that if they don't, we cannot work together. It's that important.

After they get over the initial shock of that statement, I explain that the goal revolves around their plan. The goal is that we must attempt to establish a plan that has an outcome that on the first day and every day of retirement, they will have the money to pay their bills and that they can never, ever, under any circumstance, run out of money. This needs to be the case regardless of what happens in the market, the economy, the world, or politics.

I've never had anyone not adopt that as one of their goals.

You Can't Change Yesterday

By now, the importance of comprehensive financial planning should be obvious. Even if the results are less than what you desire, it will put you on a path toward a better tomorrow. Many of us have made financial mistakes or had setbacks in the past. But that's in the past. You can't change yesterday, but you can change your tomorrow.

Regardless of your financial situation, taking this first step toward gaining the knowledge necessary to formulate your strategy for the future will inevitably put you in a better place. Having answers, good or bad, with time to act, allows you to take control and work toward the future you desire. Sticking your head in the sand and hoping for a winning lottery ticket is seldom a good financial plan.

CHAPTER 3

Who's Your Guy?

When it comes to financial advice, everyone's got a guy. It's never a girl, an advisor, or a broker. It's always a guy. Everyone's got a guy. At least, that's how it seems. Since most people have rather limited knowledge about the financial world, the markets, and planning for their future, having a guy, a financial professional, to turn to would seem to be a good thing. Or at least it should be.

Unfortunately, financial professionals use a wide range of titles and designations and are subject to different, mostly inconsistent regulatory and ethical standards. This makes it difficult, if not impossible, for the average person to understand who the players are, what they sell, what services they provide, how they are regulated, and whose best interest they have in mind. Our current regulatory system is designed to protect consumers when it comes to specifically purchasing investment products, investment advice, or insurance products. It does very little to help you decide which financial professional can provide the unbiased, comprehensive financial planning and advice you deserve to help achieve your financial goals. Because of this hole in the regulations, you must make that determination for yourself.

Titles Can Be Confusing

If you have a clogged drain, you call a plumber. It's not unreasonable to expect that any plumber who answers the call will know how to unclog your drain. That's what (most) plumbers do. The same can be expected from the electrician, carpenter, doctor, lawyer, accountant, etc. If they answer the call and show up for the appointment, they'll probably be able to provide the service you need. So who do you call if you need financial advice? A financial advisor? If it was only that simple.

In much the same way as the definition of financial planning and advice is up to the provider of the service, the titles that financial professionals use are, in many cases, equally worthless when it comes to describing the service they provide. Titles commonly used by financial professionals, such as Financial Advisor, Financial Planner, and Wealth Manager and those less commonly used - but incredibly ridiculous - such as Financial Concierge, Financial Quarterback, and Personal Chief Financial Officer, among others, are not regulated titles. The services provided by those who use these titles are up to the individual and can vary widely. According to the Securities and Exchange Commission (SEC) bulletin, *Making Sense of Financial Professional Titles,* titles may be purchased, or even made up by financial professionals hoping to imply that they have certain expertise or qualifications; such titles are generally marketing tools and are not granted by a regulator.[9]"

Titles which convey the license and registration of the financial professional, such as Investment Advisor, Registered Representative, or Insurance Producers, are regulated and will be discussed in detail in the next section.

More simply put, you have no way of knowing what a financial guy does by looking at the title on his business card. One Financial Advisor may provide comprehensive planning and multiple products, while another may only sell insurance. Once again, where the reasonable consumer should be able to make certain assumptions based on a title - after all, a plumber should be able to fix your clogged drain - no such luxury is available in the financial world. There is no way to determine, by title alone, what service someone using any financial title provides or, more important, if they are competent to provide that service.

As I write this book, the SEC and others are working on regulation to govern the use of the Advisor title.

Licenses and Registrations

The first questions you need to ask when you meet with a financial professional—or even before you meet—is what licenses do they possess? In many cases, the answer to that question will tell you what products you will be pitched. Regardless of what a financial professional may call himself, if he wants to get paid, he must possess the license and registration for the products he is selling.

There are three major players in the world of financial advice: (1) Investment Advisors or Investment Advisor Representatives, (2) Registered Representatives (broker), and (3) Insurance Producers. Each must demonstrate to a regulatory authority, through an education requirement and testing, that they are competent to sell the products covered under their license. In most cases, they must also be registered in each state they operate.

While many advisors are licensed in multiple areas, there are also many that are licensed in only one. Individuals who are licensed or registered in one area of financial advice are not required to have specific knowledge or competencies in the other areas of financial advice. More important, they are not required to take into consideration the impact of their advice or sales across other regulated or non-regulated subject areas. In other words, if your guy is a life insurance producer who possesses only a life insurance license, they are under no obligation to explain the impact of what they are selling or advising you to buy on other areas of your finances.

In fact, because they are not licensed to sell securities or give investment advice, the insurance guy cannot make recommendations regarding the purchase or sale of your investments at all! They are not obligated to analyze the impact of their advice or how it compares to other investments. Given this regulatory fact, I wonder how so many insurance guys can build their practice by executing 401(k) and IRA rollovers into annuities and other insurance products when they're prohibited from reviewing your investments.

Common sense would dictate the analysis, advice, and recommendations of an advisor who can only advise in one area may be biased toward the products or services he is licensed to sell at the expense of all others. Would you work with the same person if, instead of *Financial Advisor* or *Wealth Manager,* their business card was more honest and read *Insurance Agent* or *Stockbroker?*

There's No License Required to Give Financial Advice

Chances are when you get your haircut, the person cutting your hair has a license hanging somewhere in the shop. This lets you know that they have acquired the training necessary and have gone before a licensing authority to demonstrate that they are competent in cutting hair. The doctor, lawyer, electrician, carpenter, and plumber must also demonstrate knowledge and competence in their fields to possess the license that allows them to provide their service. So, what about the guy who gives financial advice?

Note: For the purpose of this book, I refer to *financial advice* as areas unrelated to investments or other regulated instruments. For instance, financial planning (analysis of income and expense), college planning, etc. This should not be confused with *Investment Advisor* or *investment advice*, both which are regulated and require a license.

Working with a financial professional who is licensed and registered with a federal or state authority affords the consumer certain legal protections. However, the current regulatory structure is no help in determining if someone who's holding themselves out as a financial planner, advisor, wealth manager, etc., is competent to provide comprehensive and integrated financial planning and advice. It seems ridiculous that your plumber, electrician, and the person who cuts your hair needs to be licensed and show that they can competently provide the service for which they are attempting to get paid, but the person who can do real long-term harm, the financial advisor, has no such requirement.

There is no license, test, registration, or process, from a regulatory perspective, that a financial professional must undertake to provide financial advice.

Organizations such as The American College of Financial Services and the Certified Financial Planning Board of Standards through their professional designation programs have attempted to fill the regulatory void by setting and attempting to enforce education, competency, and ethical standards for those that provide financial advice. While holders of these designations are required to show certain competencies and adhere to a high ethical standard, these organizations are not federal or state regulators. Regardless of the professional and ethical standards and rules the holders of the designation agree to uphold, there is no guarantee that the advisors will follow the rules when no one is looking. I have seen firsthand where advisors who strongly market their designation give advice that is narrow in scope and product specific. While these organizations do have the ability to discipline their designees for misbehaving, the punishment can only be within the organization - such as being forbidden from using the certification. Since these organizations are not regulatory authorities, they have no power to truly discipline an advisor.

Also, there are hundreds of designations that are available to financial professionals, some of which can be obtained by simply paying a fee. While FINRA requires that investment firms have a policy and enforcement regarding acceptable designations, the same cannot be said for many insurance producers. While some advisors feel having a long string of designations after their name conveys knowledge and authority, the truth is that it does neither. In a 2013 study, the Consumer Financial Protection Bureau (CFPB) found the use of designations to be particularly confusing to consumers, particularly seniors[10].

In most other professions, getting certifications and designations is a way of furthering one's education and staying current to developments in their field. Continuing education is an important activity of any profession. It seems that only in the world of financial professionals is the alphabet soup of designations used as a blatant marketing tool by both the holders of the designations and the organizations that sponsor them.

Be aware and very suspect of the advisor that markets using his designations. While there are certainly some designations that require extensive study and testing, implying that the advisor possesses at least an academic knowledge of a topic, It has been my experience that good advisors are good not because they possess a designation but because they have the knowledge, experience, ethics, and desire to help the clients they work with by putting their needs above the sale of a product. In my opinion, those who use their designations to convey authority, knowledge, or their superiority to other advisors, may lack them all.

Standard of Care

Written over 2,500 years ago, the principles of the Hippocratic Oath are still held sacred by physicians today. Treat the sick to the best of one's ability, preserve privacy, and never practice in areas where not qualified are just a few of the tenants of what is the ethical and legal backbone of our medical care. First, do no harm.

The inconsistencies in the regulation of financial advisors extend to the practice standards that the individual advisors must follow. Depending on the services provided, licenses and registrations held, and the products being sold, an advisor is subject to either the *Fiduciary Standard of Care or the Suitability Standard* when working with the public.

Investment Advisors, when providing investment advice, are bound to the *fiduciary standard,* which was established as part of the Investment Advisor Act of 1940. Under the fiduciary standard, Investment Advisors must:

- Work under a duty of loyalty and care by working in the client's best interest and putting the client's interests ahead of their own or that of their firm
- Disclose and avoid any potential conflicts of interest that may occur and, if unavoidable, settle them to the benefit of the client
- Act with prudence by using the skill and judgment of a professional
- Execute transactions under a *best execution* standard, meaning the advisor must strive to get the best price and execution possible.

What this means is that an Investment Advisor, when providing investment advisory service, works for you. Penalties for a breach of the fiduciary duty can be severe and may include heavy fines, jail time, or both.

Registered Representatives working for a broker-dealer and Insurance Producers are, by regulations, only required to operate under a *suitability standard.* Under a suitability standard, the advisor is simply required to know their client and their financial situation and recommend products that are suitable for their client's situation. That's all.

To be fair, while the fiduciary standard may afford customers more protection than the suitability standard, the chance of an Investment Advisor getting caught doing anything wrong is much less. While FINRA firms are audited, on average, once every 1.4 years, Investment Advisory firms average an audit every eleven years.

Under the suitability standard, a Registered Representative or Insurance Producer has no legal obligation to put the client's interest ahead of their own or that of their firm. They are not obligated to evaluate whether a competing or alternative product would be better suited for the client. Under suitability, the duty of loyalty is to the advisor's company, not to the client. In other words, these financial professionals work in the best interest of the company and not you.

Believe it or not, a financial professional can work under both standards at the same time. If you're working with an Investment Advisor who's also advising you on insurance matters, a common occurrence, the advisor will be bound by the fiduciary standard when he is giving investment advice and the suitability standard when giving insurance advice. Confused yet?

The protections of the fiduciary standard are so obvious that there are many in government and the regulatory bodies who would like to see it extended to all financial dealings with the public. In April 2016, the Department of Labor (DOL) passed a rule requiring, among other items, that any person providing advice on qualified retirement plans, including rollovers, or Individual Retirement Accounts (IRAs) act under a fiduciary standard.

In March 2018, judges from the U.S. Court of Appeals for the 5th Circuit voted to vacate the rule, ultimately killing it. Currently, as this is being written, the SEC is pondering a universal fiduciary standard covering all those involved in the sale of securities instruments.

Protection of the consumer is one area of regulation that needs an overhaul. To think that an advisor can legally put someone's financial security at risk by selling products that may be suitable but not in their best interest, just so they can get a big commission, is nuts and needs to be addressed.

One last point on the fiduciary standard: The fiduciary standard is a requirement of regulation. A person is required to act in a fiduciary capacity because of the regulations that govern their license. It is not voluntary. While some advisors may choose to act in a fiduciary manner, this does not make them a fiduciary. You can't just say you're a fiduciary. With the fiduciary standard being headline news in the industry, there are some organizations, such as the Certified Financial Planning Board, that require their members to act in a fiduciary manner or capacity. While this is commendable from an ethics perspective, it is extremely important to note that acting in a fiduciary manner is not the same as being legally bound to a fiduciary standard. I have heard some holders of the Certified Financial Planner® designation (CFP®) tell people that they are fiduciaries because they are a CFP®. This is just not true. A slap from the Certified Financial Planning Board is very different than a visit from the SEC.

Compensation

There are two primary methods by which advisors get compensated: (1) commissions and/or (2) fees. As with the standard of care, the compensation method is determined by the service offered, products being sold, and the licenses and registrations held by the advisor. In many cases, the advisor may get compensated by both fees and commission if they are acting in multiple capacities for the client.

Investment Advisors providing investment advice are generally paid a fee based on the value of assets the client has under management with the advisor. These fees will generally cover not only the services of the advisor but also trading and investment management fees. Some Investment Advisors may also charge one-time, hourly, or retainer fees for advice. All fees charged by an Investment Advisor should be clearly disclosed in an Investment Advisory Agreement signed by both the advisor and the clients.

The fee-based method of compensation is viewed as the gold-standard in financial advice since the advisor's compensation will grow by increasing the value of the assets and not by generating commissionable trades.

Registered Representatives or brokers are paid a commission for the trades they execute for their clients. Commissions can be a flat amount per trade or a percentage of the trade value, depending on the relationship and the product.

The commission structure can be different based on product type or mutual fund share class. The commissions on certain products may be paid when purchased, while others are paid at the time the product is sold. In some cases, commissions can be paid at both the purchase and the sale. While brokers are generally prohibited from charging investment fees, some products, such as certain mutual funds, can pay an upfront commission, as well as a trail commission, meaning that they receive a commission, usually monthly, for a specific period or for as long as the product is owned. Trail commissions are *hidden* inside the product and, as such, do not show up on the client's statement. While they are fully disclosed in the prospectus, I am amazed at how many people are unaware that they exist. When was the last time you read (and understood) a prospectus?

In the case of the broker, his income is derived largely by the commission he receives from the sale of securities-based products. The more he sells, the more he makes. In many cases, this commission comes *off- the-top,* meaning that it comes out of your pocket and reduces your investment amount (once again, commissions on mutual funds will vary by share class). The implication is that the broker, working under the suitability standard and being paid a commission, has an incentive to execute transactions in the client's account. How often do you get the call from your broker stating that the firm's analyst recommends selling one stock and buying another? Many people assume the broker has their best interest in mind and an expert at the firm is providing the information. This is hardly the case, yet most will agree to execute the transaction anyway.

Insurance Producers also are paid for selling products that pay a commission. These commissions are somewhat different than those earned by the broker. Where the commission paid to a broker may come off-the- top, this is not the case with most insurance products. Generally, the commission for insurance products is absorbed into the product. For example, if you invest $100,000 in a fixed annuity, $100,000 goes to work for you. Your account balance is not reduced by a commission.

Once again, common sense would dictate that you are still paying the commission (on a commission-based annuity) and it is just baked into the cost of the product.

The downside to not seeing the commission is that many insurance products can pay a very high commission to the agent. Again, under the suitability standard, the insurance guy is under no obligation to offer you the best or even lowest cost product. He simply needs to recommend a product that is suitable. Unless you are shown similar products from multiple companies, you will have no idea whether his recommendation is the best for you or him.

As the issue of compensation for advisors increases, some of the less scrupulous advisors among us have seized the opportunity to use the issue as a marketing tool. Recently, some advisors have been marketing themselves as *Fee-Only* advisors to make themselves, and their practice, appear to be superior to others. While this may seem like a good thing, we need to cut through the smoke and mirrors to see the truth.

As I previously discussed, an investment advisor who only gives investment advice - he does not recommend or sell any other products - would be a fee-only advisor since his only compensation would come from fees. Also, an advisor who only does financial planning for a fee and does not sell or recommend any product or give investment advice could also be considered a fee-only planner.

The issue I've seen is those who are yelling the loudest about being a fee-only planner or advisor are often hiding the real story. Here's another case for you to use a bit of common sense. If an advisor creates a financial plan for you that recommends some managed money (fee), and perhaps some insurance products (commission) is it conceivable that he will take the managed money and leave you to your own devices to find someone to sell you the insurance or annuity? Not likely. While there are advisors who will use fee-based annuities in this case, I personally know more than a few fee-only advisors who are a little more deceptive.

In these cases, either you will be directed to the next office, where another advisor will be more than happy to help you, or you will be informed of an affiliated company the advisor operates that handles the annuity sales. You can pretty much bet that if your advisor is insurance licensed—and perhaps even if he's not—he's getting paid. These guys are usually very easy to spot. *Fee-Only* will be a major part of their presentation and plastered all over their office and marketing materials. How your financial guy is getting paid should certainly be part of the conversation but not part of the sale.

Contrary to the fee-only mantra, paying a commission should not always be construed as a bad thing. Under certain circumstances, you may require a specific strategy or product and the fact that the advisor is getting paid a commission should not be a concern. In the case of insurance products, a one-time commission, even if it's built into the price, is far better than paying an annual fee out of your pocket for the life of the product, which could be a long time. It's far more important for you as the consumer to understand what you're paying for and whether the recommendation or transaction carries the value for the price you are paying. After all, no adviser is going to work for free.

Is Your Guy Being Held Captive?
Captive is a term used primarily in the insurance industry. Captive Insurance Producers are contracted to work for a single insurance company. In exchange for selling only that

company's policies, the insurance companies usually provide agents with a fair amount of support, possibly including an office, administrative support, and lead flow.

While structured somewhat differently, the large investment firms operate under a similar system. In exchange for services provided by the firm, which may include an office, administrative support, lead flow, investment research, and perhaps access to hard to get investment products such as Initial Public Offerings, the advisor must produce an agreed-upon level of revenue for the firm. This may come from commissions on investment products, fees from advisory business, or very often from the products or services the firm happens to be pushing that year.

Each year, *Investment News* publishes stories that contain the compensation packages for the big Wall Street firms for the following year. A few years ago, one of these articles laid out the compensation plan for the firm of a gentleman I had been trying to sit down with for quite a while. I think he was hesitant because I didn't have the *image and panache* of his big firm.

When I spoke to him early in the following year, I asked him if he was in the market for a new mortgage. He wondered why I was asking him that question since mortgages had nothing to do with what I did. I explained to him that I was curious since not only was his broker going to try to get him to refinance his mortgage, but he was also going to pitch him on private banking and a few other things that had nothing to do with his portfolio. The deal was, if I were right, we would sit down for a chat. He got the call from his broker in March, and by April he was my client.

Working with a captive means that, in many cases, the advisor will only show you products offered by that company, either because that's all the advisor can sell, or that's how he'll make his maximum compensation. While this may be acceptable and legal under a suitability standard, someone needs to explain to me how this structure can survive under a fiduciary standard as it violates most of the principles of the fiduciary duty.

As a contrast to the captive, independent advisors are usually free to sell products from a wide range of companies. As such, they should be able to show you competing products from different providers so together you can choose the product that's best for you. Even with an independent advisor, it is still vitally important that you remain diligent as incentives offered to advisors from various sources may still dictate the products they sell.

Caveat Emptor

The confusion surrounding the players in the financial advisory business, along with its share of unscrupulous and unqualified product jockeys, has a lot to do with the poor reputation of the industry. It's a contributing factor to the large number of people who try to go it alone. This is a big problem. People need comprehensive financial advice and deserve to get it without worrying about getting ripped off.

The current regulatory scheme that allows some in this industry to take advantage of the distinction between what is legal and what is ethical needs to be changed. No one should be able to screw with your money and your future just to make a buck.

Thankfully, there are many knowledgeable, qualified, and ethical financial professionals who can have a tremendously positive impact on your life. The challenge is separating the good from the bad. To do this, you must take an active role. You cannot choose a financial advisor just because they invited you to a seminar and bought you dinner.

NOTE: The appendix of this book contains a series of questions to help you interview your current or potential financial guy. How the advisor answers those questions, along with the knowledge you will gain by reading this book, should allow you to make

**a clear determination whether this guy can help you
or if he's just going to try to sell you something.**

Once armed with this information, you must act on it.
Remember, some of these guys are very good salesmen. They
are trained to overcome your objections and get you to act.
If something seems wrong, it probably is. A reputable financial professional will never need to use closing tactics or Jedi
mind tricks to get you to act. It will be a natural progression
of the planning process.

You must treat your relationship with a financial professional as a business. It's not about being friends, playing
golf, or going to the occasional dinner. Do you do these things
with your doctor? It's about you getting the financial advice
you need to achieve your goals. If that's not happening, you
must sever the relationship and find other help. Many advisors spend so much time and money on the relationship that
clients refuse to leave them, even when they are confronted
with troubling information.

I witnessed this firsthand when a family I met asked me
to review their financial plan. What they handed me to review
was their account statement - not a surprise. The statement
included various investments and a life insurance product that
neither the husband nor wife could explain. They thought they
had some insurance if the husband died, but they were not sure.

When I looked a little deeper, it turned out that their advisor, who was affiliated with one of the big national firms, had
rolled the gentleman's 401(k) into an extremely expensive and
poorly performing variable annuity. He was then taking taxable withdrawals each year to fund an expensive variable life
insurance contract that paid a benefit only after both the husband and wife died! Their retirement was being siphoned to
fund a life insurance policy that did nothing for either of them.
It must have been one heck of a commission, though. Oh, and
did I mention that, on top of everything else, they were paying
a $1,500 per year fee for a financial plan that they never got!

When faced with my review, instead of wanting to find out how to fix things, they decided to do nothing and stay with their current advisor. They explained that they had been with him for quite a while, they had been invited to his home, and they were friends. Some friend he was!

You need and deserve the financial advice that will help you achieve your goals. Understanding the players and how they operate is paramount in the search for your guy. Be educated, be diligent, and, above all, remember the advisor works for you.

CHAPTER 4

Beware of Charlatans and Snake Oil Salesmen

Access to Wall Street was once reserved for the wealthy and privileged. The high costs and expensive commissions meant that the average American was not able to participate in the game. That all changed on May 1, 1975—Mayday, as it is known on Wall Street—when the SEC allowed brokerage firms to set their commissions for executing trades. The deregulation of commissions led to the creation of discount brokers and the rise of individual investors. Not long after, in the 1980s, self-directed retirement accounts were born, and the need for the American household to participate in the market was created.

For better or worse, average Americans had the ability, regardless of their skill or knowledge, to invest their savings and retirement accounts in the market. In 1983, only 1 in 5 American families had equity investments of some type. Today, more than 50 percent of American households are invested in the market[11].

This explosion of new money has enabled the creation of the financial information and advice industry, supposedly to provide help to these new, mostly unsophisticated investors. It has become an industry that cloaks as news and education its real purpose, to separate you from your money.

The Experts and the Financial Media

Until recently, most Americans held the news media in relatively high regard. It wasn't long ago that you could sit down for 30 minutes and get the day's news. In that relatively short amount of time, by today's standards, you were given the national news, international news, local news, sports, weather, business, and usually a human-interest story. The news was the news, and the opinion, for the most part, was separate and clearly labeled as an editorial. Sure, there may have been a political slant in one direction or the other, but for the most part, we were given the facts. It was up to us to analyze the story. Back then, every story didn't include a panel of experts, as it often does today, telling us how and what we should think.

Sadly, this is no longer the case. According to The Pew Research Center's Project for Excellence in Journalism's 2013 State of the Media Report, at best 50 percent of what CNN, Fox, and MSNBC broadcast during their news programming is actually news[12]. The remainder is commentary or opinion. I would assume that these figures have gotten far worse since the 2016 presidential election. We are no longer required to think for ourselves. We get the news and are told what to think about it, all at the same time.

When it comes to politics, this constant barrage of opinion camouflaged as news is infuriating and accomplishes very little, except for giving you the ammunition you think you need to win tomorrow's political debate in the office or gym, on the bus or train, or wherever your favorite spot to *throw down* is. When it comes to the financial world, however, this type of reporting can cost the viewer dearly.

Daily, the viewers of the financial news channels are treated to a never-ending parade of so-called experts. These Economists, Market Strategists, and Investment Managers explain in language that requires an MBA to understand every tick in the market and why they think the market or a particular stock will follow their predictions. With extreme conviction, they will give us their predictions and analysis for the next day, next quarter, and next year. They also explain what you, the individual investor, should do—immediately.

Based on market conditions, they seem to trot out the same people. When the market is good, we hear from the bulls. When the market is bad, we hear from those that always think the next financial crisis is about to happen. These people are on TV, so they must know what they're talking about, right?

Does Anyone Keep Score?

Unlike most investments, there is no track record for the opinions of these prognosticators. There is no statistic like a batting average. They may be right about today, will most likely be wrong about tomorrow, and are just lucky if they are even close to their predictions for next quarter or next year. Their predictions are forgotten almost as soon as they are made, and the interviewer never questions their record. Even so, the messages from these experts are so compelling that many people will act on the information, often with disastrous results.

Here's a good example. Do a Google search on Marc Faber, Publisher of The Gloom and Doom Report, and Robert Prechter, Author and Market Analyst. Two of my favorites. They are notorious for predicting the next collapse in the market, so much so

that they often appear in the media when the market gets a little shaky.

In the case of these two, we do have statistics. Faber famously predicted a "1987 style crash" on May 10, 2012 (Dow 12,855)[13]. That's nothing new since he always predicts the market is going to crash. Prechter, who bases his predictions on a technical indicator called the Elliot Wave, predicted on July 2, 2010, that the Dow was headed to 1,000 (Dow 9,686)[14].

Today, the Dow sits above 20,000. What would have happened if you would have followed the advice of these two fear mongers every time they appeared in the media? Based on the sales of their books and newsletters, many do.

There are many more of these doomsday prognosticators that make their money with wild predictions and selling their wares to the gullible investor. Eventually, the market will crash again, and regardless of how wrong they've been for so long, they will all be out doing a victory dance and starting the cycle all over again, more popular than ever.

But what about the more reputable experts—those from the government, corporations, and Wall Street with the credentials, fancy titles, and PhDs? How do they fare?

Remember the days of the dot-com boom? Forget the fact that most of those new companies were worthless; the experts told us this was the *New Economy* where the laws of economics and the markets no longer apply. CNBC had turned the markets into a spectator sport that we had to watch and play. They trotted out the experts and told us that this time is different. There was no risk - just reward. Then the unthinkable happened. The experts were wrong, and the bubble burst.

Fast forward a few short years and things are beginning to look up. The housing market is taking off. Through the magic of financial engineering, it is now possible for anyone, regardless of income or savings, to purchase the house of their dreams. People who couldn't qualify for a mortgage on a bungalow a few years before are now purchasing a McMansion. We knew better, but the experts told us, once again, that this time is different.

For those that owned houses, this latest mania provided more equity in a short time than we thought possible. The experts enticed us to take advantage of the *free money* and build the pool, put on the addition, buy the fancy car, boat, or vacation home. After all, all this spending was good for the economy and would lead to even higher housing prices. Once again, we were told that this time is different.

At the same time, we were pouring back into the market. Our short memories and newfound wealth from our homes made us feel rich. Once again, we listened to the experts. We trusted these new fund managers that promised huge returns with little risk. New financial instruments - derivatives - would protect us. Even Alan Greenspan, Chairman of the Federal Reserve, in testimony before Congress in 2005, touted that, "The use of a growing array of derivatives and the related application of more sophisticated approaches to measuring and managing risk are key factors underpinning the greater resilience of our largest financial institutions." Joseph Cassano, head of financial products at AIG said in 2007, "It is hard for us, without being flippant, to even see a scenario within any kind of realm of reason that would see us losing one dollar in any of these [credit default] transactions."

The experts spoke, and we believed them. Maybe this time really is different. It wasn't. Once again, the experts were wrong, and we were the ones who paid the price.

I could spend chapters talking about the media's shortcomings, but I'm sure you get the point. The financial media is not your friend, and they don't exist to help you in any way. They exist to serve two purposes. First, to garner viewers and ratings to line the pockets of the network and advertisers, and second, to build the perceived authority and line the pockets of their guests, who often have paid a fee through a public relations firm to be on the air. They are not there for you! If you feel compelled to watch, please treat them as entertainment. After all, Cramer's *Mad Money* antics can be amusing.

Financial Engineering

Do you remember learning about the Scientific Method back in science class? It has been described as the best way yet discovered for separating the truth from lies and delusion. The Scientific Method is a logical and rational order of steps by which scientists come to conclusions about the world around them. That sounds pretty smart. I wonder why the Scientific Method doesn't exist in the financial world?

For those of you who were sleeping during that class, the Scientific Method requires the formulation of a hypothesis that is created through observation and tested and reformulated through experimentation. The result (if successful) is a theory that can then be open to the scrutiny of peer review - letting everyone else try to shoot holes in your shiny new theory.

The science guys have a pretty good way of doing things. Sounds like a great way to keep the crack-pots and hucksters where they belong. If your hypothesis doesn't work under ALL conditions, it just doesn't work.

Wouldn't it be nice if the investment world demanded the same methodology and scrutiny before a new financial theory or strategy was taken as gospel or a new product was sold? How many trillions of investor dollars could have been saved? While the investment world uses various methodologies for testing new products and strategies, the methods employed fall short of the rigor demanded by the Scientific Method. Unfortunately, the investment world has no (Scientific) Method.

Thanks to the financial media and our gullibility, all it takes for someone to create a new financial *law* is for someone to write an article or coin a phrase. For some reason, we are quick to accept what we hear. We may be skeptical in other areas of our lives, but when we hear of a new way to guarantee our financial success or an explanation for our current financial woes, we buy it - hook, line, and sinker. Remember the *New Economy* during the dot.com days? Or how about the *New Normal* after the 2008 financial crisis?

The world of investing is littered with can't-miss financial products that worked fine until the market for which they were designed changed. Remember the sub-prime mortgage? Worked great until interest rates ticked up and housing prices went down.

Are we facing a similar fate with the financial products and theories that have popped up since the start of this latest bull run? In early February 2018, when the Dow dropped over 1,000 points, many of the new Robo-advisors suffered website outages, preventing investors from accessing their accounts. Neither robots nor advisors, these products may work in a bull market, but have they been scrutinized under all possible market conditions? It sounds like high web traffic may be a problem! What happened to all these products that were supposed to manage our risk when the markets tanked in 2008?

What Happens When the Experts are Really, Really Wrong?

In 1994, a group of literally the smartest guys in the world of finance came together to create Long-Term Capital Management (LTCM). The group consisted of some of the best of Wall Street, academia, and even two future Nobel Prize winners. LTCM used complex mathematical models to take advantage of pricing inefficiencies in global government bond markets. Their reputations allowed them to raise over $1 billion before a trade was even made.

Things started well for LTCM. Annual returns of over 40 percent were being achieved. By the beginning of 1998, success had grown LTCM's capital from investors to $4.72 billion. To achieve these results, the firm used massive leverage, borrowing $124.5 billion. In 1998, LTCM was holding derivative positions with a notional value of approximately $1.25 trillion!

Then the unthinkable happened.

The overuse of leverage, coupled with the East Asian financial crisis of 1997 and the Russian financial crisis (and subsequent government bond default) of 1998, led to massive losses for LTCM. Somehow these brains, some of the best financial minds of the day, didn't see this coming. The effects of massive leverage, the difficulties of trading at their current size, and financial meltdown were somehow never tested in their model (or perhaps ignored). The theories used by LTCM never passed the scrutiny of the Scientific Method and, some say, came within hours of crashing the world's financial markets.

If the smartest financial minds in the world can screw up that bad, what does that say for the 10:10 AM interview on CNBC?

While a major part of LTCM's problems may have been that they just got too big, this is not the issue with much of the financial products we see today. We have short memories. The brokers who sell these products for the financial companies that develop them are quick to capitalize on that fact. Their job is to lure you with promises of something new, better, and usually exciting - and then sell. They make it hard for you to say no. After all, aren't they supposed to be the experts?

Are we doomed to repeat this pattern with every market cycle? We may find, too late, that many of the new products and investing methodologies are developed using bad math that optimizes them to the current market conditions. Unfortunately, as has been the case many times before, this will most likely lead to inevitable losses when things change. And they will change.

The Financial Televangelists and One-Size-Fits-All Advice

Dave Ramsey, Suze Orman, and other financial gurus have risen to celebrity status by giving their own brand of financial advice via TV, radio, the Internet, and through books, publications, and any other form of media they can. They have each become almost cult figures to their loyal band of followers.

While it would be easy to go on a ten-page rant about how dangerous their advice is and why you should never listen to them, that wouldn't be fair and would serve very little purpose. There are others who have already covered the subject in detail. It's more important to understand their advice - the good, the bad, and the ugly—and what impact blindly following their advice can have on your financial situation.

The Good

As an outlet for general financial advice, most have merits. Their messages revolve around being smart with your money, staying out of or getting out of debt, saving, investing, and developing good financial habits. There's nothing new or revolutionary here. It's just packaged in a way that appeals to their followers.

As I have previously discussed, financial literacy among Americans of every generation is extremely low. If these celebrities can help educate their followers, many of whom need the most help, that's a good thing. Most Americans sorely need financial education, and a strictly educational message would be a good thing. Unfortunately, that's where the good ends.

The Bad

Dave Ramsey and Suze Orman are NOT your financial advisors. While a good percentage of their advice is harmless and suitable for the masses, when they get into specifics, the problems start.

You are unique—no, not in the way your mother or third-grade teacher may have told you. You're unique financially. We all are. This may seem obvious, but how do any two individuals, who have very different financial situations, use the same advice that comes over the airwaves? Great advice for you may have devastating results for the family next door.

Both Ramsey and Orman preach that *everyone* should be in the stock market. They give specific recommendations as to the instruments you should invest in. In Ramsey's case, his blatant disregard for, or ignorance of, basic financial math makes his recommendations seem much better than they are.

As far as Orman's investment recommendations are concerned, this is where it gets troubling. For the longest time, Suze would steer listeners into the Vanguard's S&P 500 Fund. Not a horrible choice for part of a portfolio, but it shouldn't be your only investment. Somehow this advice has gotten mistaken by some of her listeners as simply *buy Vanguard.*

On more than a few occasions, I have reviewed portfolios which contained nothing but Vanguard products. That's not unusual, but when I inquired as to the rationale of the choices, the response was, "Suze Orman said buy Vanguard." My next, obvious, question was, "Okay, but why these funds?" Almost predictably the answer came back, "Suze Orman said buy Vanguard."

Now, to be fair, I'm not aware of Suze giving this advice, although I've heard this pearl of wisdom on many occasions from the free advice crowd. Don't get me wrong; Vanguard is an excellent company with many good products. Their goal is to provide a quality product at an extremely low expense level. So "buy Vanguard" seems like good advice.

Here's the issue. Vanguard currently has over 200 products that are available to their retail customers, online with the click of a mouse. Selecting the proper investment for your needs takes a heck of a lot more than just buying Vanguard. Also, low cost or cheap doesn't always ensure the best performance. If it did, Vanguard's products would always be the best performing. The truth is, they hardly make it to the top of the performance lists. The reality is that when you include other factors in an analysis, simple, often self-serving, advice doesn't tell the whole story. Price should only be a factor where all else is ignored or where all products are the same. This is seldom true in the investment world.

How can this generic advice possibly be a good thing? While being in the market may be good advice for many, what about the family that's living pay- check-to-paycheck with no savings? If they can scrape together a few dollars per month for savings, should they pour it into a mutual fund or perhaps be better served to keep it in a bank account for an emergency?

Dave or Suze have never met you. Even if you're lucky enough to call into one of their shows, they still know next to nothing about your situation. How can any advice they give be of any value, and how would that advice change if they were able to, or wanted to, take the time to find out your story?

The only reason they can give any investment advice at all is that they are not licensed. If I gave this type of generic advice without knowing anything about the person I was giving it to, I would lose my license. And I should.

The Ugly

Everybody is selling something. That's certainly the case with the financial celebrities. I don't have an issue with this. If you look at many of the books, DVDs, and guides put out by this group, you may find some nuggets of good information, as long as you understand that you cannot blindly apply it to your situation. In Orman's case, she has published *kits* on such things as improving your credit score and creating wills. While this information could be found for free if you took the time to search the Internet, you could probably say that about most topics.

The problem starts when they use their celebrity status and the loyalty of their followers to sell other products. Dave Ramsey pushes listeners to his list of Endorsed Local Providers (ELPs) who pay a fee to be included on the list. While the website states that there is an interview process that takes place before someone can become an ELP, one would have to assume that the advisors who are working under this relationship will be pushing Ramsey's recommendations. What happens if the financial advisor does his job and finds that Ramsey's advice is not what's best for this person? (Notice I didn't say suitable - as we've seen, it can be suitable under the standard but still not best for the client.) Can they do the right thing, or are they bound to follow Ramsey's advice?

In 2012, Suze Orman used her celebrity status and followers to push a now-defunct pre-paid debit card. The *Advantage Card* was touted as being able to improve the cardholders FICO score. As it turned out, the only credit agency involved,

TransUnion, agreed only to "examine the data." The card was expensive and unable to produce the FICO results, hurting the very people that could least afford it. It was quietly discontinued in2014.

Both Ramsey and Orman preach the philosophy of - *buy term and invest the difference* - when it comes to life insurance. While my issue is not with the philosophy - I'll get into that discussion in more detail in chapter 13 - my issue is that Orman is a spokesperson for SelectQuote, an online insurance quote engine. I have reviewed many policies for new clients that had gone through SelectQuote. In many of the cases, the policy that was ultimately purchased was much more expensive and often not even the same policy that was applied for. These were people without health or other issues that would cause a rating issue with a policy.

What Suze fails to tell her audience is that a term policy may cost the same purchased online or through an independent agent. I often compare prices for term insurance that I obtain direct from the carriers with those from the online sources and see little if any difference. Flying solo, a consumer is left to his own devices.

Insurance can be confusing. How much does the average consumer really understand? I would never let a client get pushed into a more expensive and less beneficial policy. They are at risk of this bait-and-switch because they don't know enough to advocate for themselves with the insurance company. Suze should know that since she sold insurance when she was an advisor. Does she really believe *buy term and invest the difference?* Or, can she make more money giving that advice now? Hard to tell. After all, she made a lot of money selling cash value life insurance in her days as an advisor.

Are you a Reasonable Person?
We all think we're reasonable people. The government might think otherwise. When the Department of Labor drafted their Fiduciary Rule, there was much discussion over how to treat

those who gave financial advice to the public, over the airwaves, and in print, all the people I discussed in this chapter. Many in the industry feel that generic advice should be subject to the same rule as financial advisors. After all, millions follow their advice. The Department of Labor felt otherwise. According to the DOL, and included in the now defunct ruling, *advisors are explicitly exempted from the best-interest standard for communications that "a reasonable person would not view as an investment recommendation," such as general-circulation newsletters; television, radio and talk show commentary; and generally attended speeches and conferences*[15]

Let me decode that for you. It means if you ever followed the advice that the experts on the financial media, the financial celebrities, the local advisors with radio shows, the doomsday newsletter writers, or anyone else who writes, talks, or gives advice in a public forum, you are not a reasonable person, since a reasonable person wouldn't do this. Therefore, they are not subject to the rule and do not have to act in the best interest of those they are advising.

Put more simply, it means that the very people whose livelihood depends on you doing dumb things with your money are exempt from the very rule that's supposed to protect you from doing dumb things with your money. Go figure. Let's hope the SEC does a better job.

Technology has given these experts, pundits, gurus, prognosticators, and product jockeys a pulpit from which to peddle their goods. We should know better; but somehow when it comes to money, our common sense often goes out the window. How many billions of dollars have Americans shelled out for weight loss solutions? While we hope for miracles from these magic pills and gadgets, the answer was right in front of us all the time. Want to lose weight? Eat well and exercise. Want to achieve your financial goals? Create, execute, and follow a financial plan. There are no shortcuts.

Just because someone says something with authority, conviction, and volume, it doesn't make it true.

Chapter 5

You Are Not a Trader!

WARNING: This chapter may offend some of you. If it does, please read it again. It most likely applies to you!

Just because you can, doesn't mean you should.

Great advice under most circumstances - indispensable advice when it comes to investing. Unfortunately, far too few people heed this simple advice.

Back in the days of the dot-com boom, everyone wanted to be a trader. Why not? The market was going up almost every day, and all you had to do was buy the latest dot-com stock and hang on. Making money seemed so easy. Spurred on by the financial media, people with no knowledge or experience in finance or the markets were quitting their day jobs to pursue the seemingly quick riches and easy life of a day trader. The brokerages told us it was easy. Use their tools and trading platform, and we were sure to make our fortune.

Unfortunately for those looking to take easy money from the market, things there work very much like the casino. Just because you're allowed to go to the casino and play poker doesn't mean you're a professional gambler or that you can compete with a professional. More than likely, they'll welcome you to the table, take your hard-earned money, direct you

55

to the ATM to get some more, and then take that, too. At least in Vegas, you might get some show tickets and a seafood buffet as a parting gift. The market works pretty much the same way, except you don't get to see Celine Dion and gorge yourself on crab legs to ease the pain of losing your shirt. No amount spent on day trading books and courses can change that.

The dot-com bubble, as all bubbles eventually do, burst. With it went the hopes, dreams, and bank accounts of the day traders. These new traders, who knew next to nothing about trading, couldn't make a penny when the market wasn't going up every day. When things got difficult, as they always will, they had no idea what to do. There's a saying in the trading world: **trading is simple, not easy!** Trading is hard, guys.

Today's self-directed IRAs, brokerage accounts, and defined contribution retirement plans require you to make investment decisions that could impact the rest of your life. These decisions require careful thought, specific knowledge, analysis, and the conviction and discipline to follow a trading plan. Successful investing is difficult, and the average investor is just not that good at it.

The Emotional Cycle (or is that Rollercoaster) of Investing

The field of Behavioral Finance attempts, among other things, to understand and explain why individuals behave the way they do when it comes to personal finance and investing and, more important, what causes poor decision making. Most modern theories that attempt to explain the actions of the markets are built on the assumption that investors think and act rationally. Behavioral Finance assumes that most investors act irrationally and make investment decisions based on emotion. Sounds about right to me.

The average investor's decisions are usually driven by overconfidence, ego, and emotion. Overconfidence in our knowledge and abilities, combined with a smattering of ego, makes you think you can *play the market.* I cringe every time I hear someone say those words. Once in the market, emotions take over. Instead of following a trading plan as the professionals do, the emotions of fear, greed, hope, and despair dictate your actions. Emotions rule the individual investor, often with devastating results.

Buy low and sell high. Classic investing wisdom. What makes more sense than buying when things are cheap and selling when they get expensive? However, this is seldom what the inexperienced do. According to the 2014 *Quantitative Analysis of Investor Behavior* (QAIB), an annual report published by DALBAR, emotions, which cause investors to do the wrong things at the wrong times, have caused the average investor to underperform the long-term results of the markets.

> "...we have learned that the greatest losses occur after a market decline. Investors tend to sell after experiencing a paper loss and start investing only after the markets have recovered their value. The devastating result of this behavior is participating in the downside while being out of the market during the rise.[16]"

This pattern has been repeated countless times. Investors are on the sidelines as the market starts to climb. As it climbs higher, optimism takes hold and, not wanting to be left out, more people pile in. Soon, as optimism turns to excitement and then to exuberance, those still on the sidelines pour into the market. The financial media and the pundits cheer the markets to new highs. Everyone, including the experts, think the market will go up forever. And then it's over.

As the market starts on the downward side of the cycle, investors are in denial. This wasn't supposed to happen. Denial turns to fear, then desperation. Investors head for the exits in droves. For those remaining, panic sets in and more exit. The experts are now saying that this is the big one—another 2008 or even worse. Finally, capitulation, when those that have tried so hard to hang on finally give up in a final wave of selling. And then it's over. The market has hit bottom.

As the market starts to climb, those who have sold everything remain on the sidelines. It will be a long time before the optimism returns and they feel safe to enter the market once again.

Emotions result in irrational investment decisions. Irrational decisions rarely give good results.

Even though the era of the day trader may be over - for now - many people are still making investment decisions and managing their portfolios with the same short-term, beat-the-market mentality. Why do so many people, with no understanding of business, finance, investments, or math - many of whom can't even balance their checkbook - think they can make complex investment decisions?

The investing public operates under a set of false assumptions that convince them that they need, and are qualified, to make these complex investment decisions. These assumptions are based on information provided by the very people who gain the most from irrational and emotional decision making - the financial media and the brokerages. Hopefully, understanding and debunking these assumptions can prevent, in my opinion, the single biggest detriment to achieving your financial goals—the uncanny ability to do dumb things with your money!

Assumption 1: You Can Beat the Market

The idea that investors - individual or professional - can beat the market on a regular basis has become a common theme. This myth is spread by the financial media as it gets viewers to tune in and helps sell their advertisers' products. The brokerage industry alludes to its possibilities to get you to churn your account with trades, allowing them to collect vast sums of commission dollars. An entire advice industry is based on the premise, encouraging you to trade your dollars for their newsletters, websites, trade recommendations, and instructional classes, all designed to make it possible for you to beat the market.

Is it possible to consistently beat the market? First, we need to understand what that even means.

The commonly accepted definition of beating the market refers to the average working American obtaining a higher *total return* for a given period than the S&P 500 Index. While I would argue that the S&P 500 is a poor representation of the total market as it only represents a narrow swath - large-cap stocks - since most people think it's the market, let's go with that.

Here lies the first problem. Investors are already starting at a deficit. The S&P 500, or any index, is simply a calculation of the combined prices of the underlying instruments. It does not consider the costs associated with making or managing the investment. Your total return on any investment must include all commissions, fees, and taxes that are attributable to the investment. None of these are included in the index that you are trying to beat. The more you trade, the more it costs, the harder it will be to outperform an index.

The performance of individual investors is not good. The 2017 QAIB found that for the 30-year period ending 12/31/16, the average equity mutual fund investor underperformed the S&P 500 by more than 6 percentage points annually[17].

A January 2017 report by CNBC showed how, in 2016, the 70,000 people who tracked their portfolio on the *Openfolio* social network generated an average gain of roughly 5 percent. This trailed the nearly 12 percent return of the S&P 500 by 7 percentage points[18].

Proponents of indexing or *passive investing* use these figures as proof that *active investing* is fruitless. Active versus passive investing is a heated, ongoing debate in the investment world and one I'll settle later.

I could fill these pages with the results of studies and analysis that all come to the same conclusion. Beating the market on a consistent basis is not something the average investor or even the professional can do. However, it doesn't stop people from trying.

To capture *alpha,* the percentage of excess return greater than the index, investors resort to risky and self-defeating strategies, such as attempting to time the market or investing in portfolios that are heavily concentrated in only a few stocks. While these tactics may work for the very short term, luck should never be confused with skill. That usually ends badly.

If the evidence is overwhelming that attempting to beat the market is a fool's game, why do so many people try? Perhaps it's overconfidence, ego, or just a desire to play. I have a better question: Why do you think you need to beat the market?

Assumption 2: You Need to Beat the Market

Successful investing starts with reasonable expectations. What happens when someone's expectations are not reasonable, and their entire investment strategy is based on unobtainable or unnecessary goals? Usually, bad things follow.

Unlike those who think their investing savvy will allow them to beat the market consistently, those who think they need to beat the market are usually not aware of what they are doing. For these people, for reasons that can be directly linked to the lack of a plan, they have either an unreasonable expectation for the money they need to attain their goals or an irrational expectation of a reasonable rate of return. Both misconceptions can needlessly lead to unwelcome results.

Before I begin to work with a prospect, they are asked to complete a Risk Profile Questionnaire that I developed. One of the questions I ask is: **What would you consider to be a reasonable or target (goal) annual rate of return for your investment portfolio?** Most people give an answer in a reasonable range for discussion of 4 percent to 10 percent.

A prospect I spoke with recently answered that question with a target return of 100 percent. I assumed this was a mistake and that he didn't understand the question. When I reviewed the questionnaire with him and questioned him about his response, he stated that he indeed needed to double his money every year. That was the only way his $40,000 account would be worth the $1 million he thought he needed for retirement. When I asked if he thought that was reasonable, or even possible, he stated that it didn't matter. That's what he needs.

I'm pretty sure there's no need for me to explain the absurdity of his response. While that's an extreme example, many people think that 12 percent, 15 percent, or even 20 percent are reasonable rates of return. While the market may give those returns in any given year, the chance of achieving those returns, as an average, over any length of time is nuts. Once again, the question I must ask is, *what are you thinking?*

In a similar case, I met a woman a little while back who was looking to get a better handle on her retirement plan. She was in her early 50s, single, had no debt and very low expenses. A pretty good financial situation. She had a $500,000 portfolio, invested in various Vanguard products, all extremely high on the risk scale.

When I asked about her portfolio, she explained that she didn't think she had enough money to retire at this point. Since she still had 10 to 15 years before retirement, I didn't see much of an issue. There was no real reasoning behind the holdings, except the woman's intention to take as much risk as possible because she didn't have enough.

I asked her the obvious question. "How do you know you don't have enough?" All she would divulge is that she figured it out. She would not share her plan or calculations or even admit where she was getting her information.

A quick analysis, based on the information she would divulge, showed she would have more than enough money to retire with her current savings rate. She could drastically reduce the risk in the portfolio and still have more than enough money to live retirement the way she envisioned.

It wasn't long until we realized that we weren't a good fit. She insisted that her free advice was working out well (guess who she was listening to?). I wished her well and sent her on her way. Hopefully, when the next big correction in the market happens, her generic, free advice will work out.

Both stories have a common theme. Their actions are directly attributable to not having gone through the financial planning process. Lack of planning—and listening to free advice—caused them to focus solely on investing and returns.

Most of you reading this book probably don't have a financial plan. If you do, it probably isn't a good one. After all, if you were all buttoned up financially, why would you be reading this book?

Investing in a vacuum will most likely end badly. It's all fun and games when the market goes up every day. What happens to your goals when the market doesn't cooperate and returns are harder to come by, if at all? Do you have a plan to follow, or do you stick your head in the sand until the scary stuff is over? Hitting your financial target is impossible if you have no idea what you're shooting at.

Assumption 3: So Easy a Baby Can Do It

Between my days in the corporate world and the time spent running my own companies, I have amassed over 30 years of finance and financial markets experience. In that time, I have worked on taking companies public, joint ventures in China, managing a large pension fund, developing currency hedging programs, and a whole host of corporate finance tasks. I have developed trading strategies, run a currency hedge fund, and manage the retirement plans and assets for the families I currently work with. I have a master's degree in International Finance, and I am a Chartered Financial Consultant®. I say all this not to brag or impress you with my resume but to show the depth of my experience. I've been at this a while. For all I have done, there is always more to learn. Always new topics, instruments, and regulations to understand. This is my career.

It amazes and at the same time infuriates me that the financial media and the brokerages have led people to think this stuff is so simple that anyone can do it. Is this why so many people have troubles admitting they just don't understand? Just as it's ridiculous to think that you can perform an appendectomy on yourself with nothing more than WebMD, a copy of Gray's Anatomy, and an X-Acto knife, is it any less ridiculous to think you can become an investment expert by doing nothing more than trolling the web and watching Cramer?

It's equally ridiculous to think you should be an expert. Would you try to fake your way through a discussion on astrophysics? Unless you had a background in science, math, or some similar discipline, I must assume you would think it's not a sign of weakness to ask questions. After all, that stuff is difficult, and there's no reason for anyone to think you would or should understand.

Somehow, though, when the conversation turns to the markets and investing, people just can't admit they don't understand. I call these people **Bobbleheads** since, no matter what I say, they just sit and nod in agreement.

The loudmouth braggart is convinced that they know it all; they make their own investment decisions, then brag only about the few winners, and ignore all else. In contrast, the Bobblehead can't admit they don't understand the concept or product. They won't ask the important questions and end up buying financial products they don't understand or need. I see it all the time. Often, when reviewing a prospect's financial holdings, they have no idea why they purchased some financial product. I will never let a client or prospect get away with being a Bobblehead. I won't allow any transaction to be done if I'm not convinced of their understanding. Unfortunately, that's not how most people operate in this business. Bobbleheads are easy marks to many advisors who talk in financial jargon simply to impress and confuse.

I have a friend who was a Bobblehead. He would never admit he was clueless about financial matters. He loved to talk about the markets and investing and actively trading in his 401(k). As a Contractor, he spent quite a bit of time on the road. He used that time to listen to copious amounts of financial talk radio.

I was out at dinner with two friends, who are also advisors. We were meeting the Contractor. These guys thought the Contractor was fairly knowledgeable about the markets and investing. I was so convinced he was a Bobblehead I made the two advisors a wager. Before our Contractor friend arrived that night, I bet them that I could talk financial gibberish to him for 30 minutes and he would only sit there and nod. He would agree with everything I said, the true test of a Bobblehead.

For 30 minutes, I strung together nothing but disjointed thoughts, made-up phrases, and complete nonsense. Not once could he bring himself to admit he had no idea what I was talking about. As ridiculous as it was, it demonstrated that, for whatever reason, people feel it necessary to be an expert in something they're obviously not. My winnings for the night - a $50 steak and a few single malts. Not too bad.

Finance, investing, and understanding the market and economy require a specialized knowledge that can only come from education and experience. No amount of Internet education is going to make you an expert. If you're not an expert, it's okay. You don't need to be. Just have the confidence to ask questions.

Assumption 4: It's Not Marketing; It's Education

The brokerages and big financial firms are masters of marketing. They can make you feel like you're not being marketed to but, instead, being educated. Remember the day traders? It was the marketing of the brokerages that convinced so many people that it was easy. The commercials combined just a dash of education with images of trading screens complete with their trading tools, dramatic music, and shots of happy men and woman spending the day in front of their computer screens. You saw a way to make easy money. The brokerages saw it as an even easier way to make money - get you to trade, a lot. How did that work out?

Today, the brokerages are using similar tactics to get you to execute trades. A little education sprinkled in with their marketing. As an example, in a recent E*TRADE commercial, the spokesman is walking through a town with a woman who is noticing all the bearded millennials walking around. The topic is trends.

Spokesman: You, my friend, recognize when a trend has reached critical mass. When others focus on one thing, you see what's coming next. You see opportunity. That's what a Type E does.

With that, a guy walks out of a barbershop, rubbing his cleanly shaven face.

Spokesman: And so, it begins.

So, what's the implication? That because one guy shaved off his goofy looking beard that suddenly everyone was going to shave? Time to buy stock in Gillette? Maybe his wife just threatened him that if he didn't shave that ugly thing off his face, she was going shopping, a lot. **THAT'S NOT THE WAY IT WORKS!** Stop doing stuff like that.

There's a big difference between education and advertising. You should all know this; however, when it comes to the world of investing, many of us forget.

According to Miriam-Webster, education, or by extension learning, is the activity or process of gaining knowledge or skill by studying, practicing, being taught, or experiencing something. On the other hand, advertising is a form of marketing communication used to encourage, persuade, or manipulate an audience to take or continue to take some action. That's a big difference.

We all know that an infomercial is just a commercial designed to make you think you are learning something so you buy the product. If you think of the commercials of the financial firms as nothing more than infomercials, you may look at the content differently and not be persuaded by the ridiculous message. Better yet, treat them as entertainment. Some of them are pretty funny.

It's important to remember that brokerage firms primarily make money with your money. The more of it they have, the more money they make. It's a pretty safe bet that the more they educate you, and the more you think you know, the more you'll give them. Good for their bottom line, maybe not so good for yours.

Assumption 5: This is a Good Investment Because I Know the Company/Industry

One of the most financially dangerous traps people fall into in the world of investing is getting emotionally attached to a stock. Do you have a stock in your portfolio that you would never think of selling under any condition? Perhaps they are shares of a company you work for, or maybe you were given the shares by a parent or grandparent as a gift. Some people even purchase shares of a company in an industry that they are interested in, thinking that their knowledge gives them an advantage.

Anytime you get emotionally attached to an investment, your judgment gets clouded. Often when this happens, you will disregard any negative reports on your stock or industry and instead focus only on the positive. You forget the main purpose of owning the stock. It's not about sentiment. It's about the return.

If an investment represents too large a proportion of your total portfolio, you are putting your financial future at undue risk. This is especially true if you work for the company. Many companies make it very attractive for employees to purchase stock. In these companies, you can purchase the stock at a discount in an Employee Stock Purchase Plan and own shares in your 401(k). I have seen many people who have great confidence in their companies max out their contributions to both plans, making their holding of that one stock a very large percentage of their total portfolio. This can lead to a nightmare scenario if the company falls on hard times and the stock price tanks. Worse yet, the company folds or institutes layoffs, and you lose your job. Think Enron, WorldCom, Lucent, and so many others. Employees who drank the company Kool-Aid may have a large amount of their life savings invested in the company they work for and then POOF - it's all gone.

There are very few people in a company who know the true financial story of the company, and I can pretty much guarantee that you're probably not one of them. Even the Wall Street analysts can only ascertain so much about a company. They are certainly more knowledgeable than most (non-financial) employees but, far from perfect. If they were, how come there are always *earnings surprises?*

Good companies are good - until they're not. By the time you realize there's a problem, it will most likely be too late. Remember Lucent? The analysts kept saying it would come back, but it never did.

Any investment, regardless of how you came to own it, is just a tool to get a return. A stock may have been a great investment when your grandfather worked for the company, but we live in a much different world, different economy. GM stock was held by generations and treated like a treasured family possession. Then the financial crisis happened. Would granddad have wanted you to ride that stock into the ground?

Regardless of what you think you know about a company, your information is of extremely limited value because everyone has it. You own that stock for only one reason: to get a return. The minute you get sentimental about an investment, for whatever reason, you open yourself up to undue risk that you otherwise would probably never take.

Assumption 6: I Can Do the Analysis and Make Good Decisions

How are you doing with your investments? Seems like a pretty simple question. Just calculate the return. If you can make complex investment decisions, you should be able to figure out how you're really doing. This should be a rather simple matter. Unfortunately, most people are notoriously bad at math.

Any time I give a presentation to a group, I always start by asking the same question: *How did you do in the market last year?* Lately, the answers vary from good to great to spectacular! When the market is good, this always gets the room smiling. Not willing to leave it there, I always follow up with: *How do you know?* There go the smiles.

Most people judge their investment performance by simply looking at their year-end statement. Is the year-end account balance on December 31st greater than the January 1st balance at the beginning of the year? Great, you had a good year. There are obvious problems with this type of thinking. It doesn't come close to telling the entire story.

Let's say that you could do the math and found you had an 8 percent return for the past year. The market returned 10 percent. Did you have a good year? Well, it depends.

If your portfolio is moderately invested in a diversified portfolio of stocks and fixed-income investments, then you probably had a good year. If, on the other hand, you're invested in a concentrated portfolio of high-risk stocks, you had a terrible year! Sometimes the answer is a little more complex than just dividing two numbers. Just looking at the beginning and ending balances is a horrible way to judge performance. More on this topic later.

Remember the Contractor that liked to trade his 401(k)? He was under the impression that he was doing very well over the past ten years or so. When I reviewed his statements, I had some hard news for him to hear. He was figuring his performance by looking at how his balance had grown. Seems like a valid assumption, right? Well, not really. You see the balance numbers he was looking at included his contributions. When I backed out all the contributions for those years, his actual returns were rather abysmal.

How about the performance of that last stock you sold? How do you know how you did there? The calculations are not as simple as they seem on the surface. To illustrate the issue, let's first look at a simple profit calculation on the purchase and sale of a house:

Purchase price: $450,000

Sale Price: $650,000

What's the profit? Must be $200,000, right? Not even close! What about closing costs, both on the purchase and the sale. And what about all the renovations you did? There's a bunch of stuff that goes into calculating the final profit or loss. If you paid $450,000 for the house, had $50,000 in closing and realtor fees, and did $100,000 in renovations, your actual profit is only $50,000, not $200,000! It's probably even less. I only included the big items.

The initial cost of the house plus all these added costs is the adjusted basis of the house. When calculating your profit, you need to subtract the adjusted basis from the sale price to get your true profit.

Now let's look at stock. Let's say you bought 100 shares of XYZ Corp. for $10.00 per share and then sold them a year later for $12.00 per share. I guess you already figured the profit isn't $2.00 per share. You need to calculate the adjusted basis of the stock, which includes the commissions and fees, and subtract that from the sale price. Oh, and don't forget the taxes that will be due on the profit. The tax due will vary based on the holding period. Not so simple, is it?

Another area where many people get confused is calculating annual returns. Here's a simple one:

Year 1: The market return is -50 percent

Year 2: The market return is +50 percent

What's the total return for the two-year period? A quick glance would seem to tell us that if we lost 50 percent in year 1 and made 50 percent in year 2 that our return for the two years was zero percent. Should be back to where we started. Nope! The correct answer is -25 percent.

How's that, you ask? While you lost 50 percent of $100,000 (or $50,000) the first year, the gain the second year was only 50 percent of $50,000 (or $25,000). This leaves you at a loss of $25,000 over the two years or 25 percent.

This simple math tripped up a few commentators after the events of 2008. In 2008, the S&P (including dividends) lost roughly 37 percent. The index was up approximately 26.5 percent in 2009 and 15 percent in 2010, prompting more than a few commentators and supposed intelligent individuals to conclude that the market had recovered its losses. It didn't, and now you know why. It took until early 2013 for the S&P to get back to its pre-2008 highs.

I hope you get the point. Even simple math is not so simple if you don't have all the information.

One of the costliest mistakes I see individuals make is basing the decision of when to cash in a profit on the tax that will be due on the profit. No one wants to pay tax, but taxes are a cost of doing business. People who trade for a living are aware of this. There's pretty much only one way not to pay tax (assuming the investment is in a taxable account), and that's to take a loss. Paying tax is a good thing. It means you made money!

I discovered just how much this tax issue could affect people. Shortly after Lucent tanked, I met an attorney from Lucent at a dinner party. During our discussion, he told me that, at its peak, he had $7.5 million in Lucent stock options that he could have exercised (cashed in.) I thought I would ask the obvious question. How much did he exercise? His response shocked me beyond belief. He didn't cash in any, at any point. His reason was that he didn't need the money right now and he didn't want to pay the tax. What did he get for all those options? Nothing!

Making investment decisions in a vacuum will almost never yield the right answer. If instead of basing his decision on the amount of tax he would need to pay, he analyzed his decision in conjunction with his financial plan and his family's financial goals, how might his decision be different? Even if he only netted $3.5 million, after taxes, what would that mean to his retirement? Would he and his wife be able to retire earlier, buy a house on the beach, travel more? The true cost of his decision may go well beyond the dollars lost.

Assumption 7: It's Okay to Play Since it's in My IRA

Many people think their bad trading decisions are somehow less bad because the investment is sitting in their IRA. They have no problem buying the latest hot tip from the guy they overhear at Starbucks or buying into the latest penny stock scam email they received. Why not swing for the fences?

Because of the long-time horizon of the IRA, they can some how justify sitting on a speculative stock that plummeted, mentally labeling it as a long-term holding, hoping it will come back. It won't. The only difference between your IRA/401(k) and taxable accounts is that there is no immediate tax implication in the retirement account. Your bad decision is still a bad decision. Now it will just affect your retirement.

Does your spouse know how your trading habit is affecting your future? Probably not. No, it's not all right!

Still, Think You're a Trader?

Contrary to what the financial media, the pundits, and the brokerages would like you to think, the markets are not easy. Being successful takes knowledge, time, and emotional discipline that very few individuals possess. I hope this chapter helps you see that. There's more to being successful than just listening to the pontifications of the 10:10 AM interview on CNBC or following some guru's recommendations.

If these people actually knew something that no one else did, they certainly wouldn't share it with you. For me, if I knew where the market was going, with 100 percent certainty, I'd be on a beach somewhere sipping a tropical drink. No one knows what's going to happen next, and anyone who tries to convince you otherwise is either a liar or, more likely, trying to sell you something.

The secret to good investing is remembering why you do it. You want financial success and the ability to achieve your goals. Eliminating destructive market behavior is as simple as creating and following a plan. As Mike Tyson famously said, "Everyone has a plan until they get punched in the face." It's at those exact times, when the market punches you in the face, that you need a plan the most.

If it's true that emotions cause investors to do the wrong things at the wrong times and volatility in the market causes investors to be emotional, you must find a way to control your emotions. The only way to do that is to have a plan and the discipline to follow it. Having a good advisor to talk you off the ledge, if needed, doesn't hurt, either.

For those of you who still want to play the market, my suggestion is to open a small account and have at it. The only rule is that the small amount of funds you commit are all you get. Blow out the account, and you'll need to find another drug, I mean, hobby.

The next time you go to make that questionable investment, remember, no message pops up on the screens asking: *Are you sure you want to put your entire retirement in THAT?*

CHAPTER 6

Risk: It's Much More Than You Think

I am a risk manager. That's my ultimate role for the families I serve in my practice. Sure, I manage their investments, insurance, financial plans, and a whole manner of other items. But my primary function is to assist my clients in dealing with risk.

Risk is one of the most misunderstood and complex topics in the financial world. There are many books written that focus solely on the topic, by individuals who dedicate their entire careers to understanding and attempting to find ways to manage or eliminate it. However, the simplistic, readily available information on the Internet and in the media leaves us with a sense that we have a good understanding of the topic. Unfortunately, as with many other financial topics, misconceptions and oversimplifications can have disastrous effects.

In my first meeting with a family, I always engage them in a conversation about risk. As part of the conversation, I will ask them to define what risk means to them with regard to their financial life. While the answers I get may differ slightly from family to family, in every case (yes, 100 percent), their answer is that risk is the possibility that their investments will lose value. In other words, market risk.

This is not surprising. After all, we are conditioned early on to believe that risk is synonymous with the market. In fact, most conversations I hear about risk focus strictly on the market.

Unfortunately, many advisors focus specifically on market risk since they know you are keenly aware of it and that it probably makes you nervous. The stock jockey may spend a tremendous amount of time showing you charts, graphs, and mathematical formulas to try to get you to understand something for which they, in many cases, have little or no understanding; the insurance guy will spend his time exploiting your fear and trepidation.

By focusing the risk conversation strictly on market risk, financial advisors - and many do-it-yourselfers— are leaving gaping holes in financial plans. These holes will most likely lead to unwelcome surprises when you're least able to do anything about them.

Then What is Risk?

Risk is hardly a simple subject. In fact, risk is one of the most complex areas of finance and one that's thoroughly understood by very few financial advisors. Here lies the problem. The industry has attempted to dumb down the subject into tidbits that the practitioners can explain, and the public can understand. There's much more to the subject of risk than most people are aware.

Risk is not some abstract concept, as it is often presented. It is, in many cases, quantifiable where its effects can be measured and managed.

Risk can be defined in many ways. In its purest form, risk can be defined as uncertainty. From a financial standpoint, other than a possibility of a loss, risk can be defined as the possibility of an event occurring that will give an undesired outcome. In plain English, risk is the possibility, or probability, that something will go wrong, preventing you from achieving your financial goals.

In this chapter, in addition to market risk, I will delve into other, more important areas of risk, including the big three: inflation, longevity, and something called sequence of returns.

Market Risk

Since so much time, ink, and attention is spent on market risk, let's start there. Market risk is simply a fact of life. Unless you have all your money in a bank account or stuffed in your mattress (or various other *safe investments),* there will always be some degree of market risk involved.

With regard to market risk, we are taught from an early age about the relationship between risk and return. The assumption is that the greater the risk, in the markets or life, the greater the rewards. No guts, no glory, as the saying goes. While this adage may have some truth from a purely academic standpoint, we must quantify what is meant by risk. Unfortunately, as with most of the adages in the financial world, the concept of risk and reward has become analogous with being greedy or just plain reckless.

For example, how many times have you heard that you should take more risk when you're younger because there's plenty of time to recover from a loss? More risk leads to potentially more reward, right? The problem becomes when taking a measured risk - a higher allocation to equities, for example - is confused with day trading your IRA or investing in the latest gas and oil drilling scheme that was advertised on TV.

I would argue that if we took a more measured approach and looked at retirement savings as a marathon rather than a sprint, we would be much better off.

What's Your Risk Profile?

Financial regulations mandate that before a financial professional can open an account or sell you any product, they must establish and understand your risk tolerance. This ensures the product or investment they are selling is suitable for you and within the risk level you are willing to take. This is also true if you open any type of investment account or buy a financial product over the Internet or the phone.

In many cases, risk tolerance is established by the financial professional or website simply asking whether you *feel you are conservative, moderate, or aggressive.* In some instances, they may add an extra level of *precision* (italics here denote sarcasm) by including the categories of *moderately conservative and moderately aggressive.* This single question is all that is required by regulation and may encompass the entire risk discussion in establishing your account. Your answer will determine the allocation of your portfolio and the financial products you will be sold.

For many advisors, this is as far as the discussion will go, either because they don't understand risk or that's all they are required to do to sell you their product.

I'm sure most readers understand the concept of risk tolerance. Some of us are more comfortable engaging in activities others perceive to be risky. Most would agree that activities such as skydiving, car racing, and bungee jumping are high risk and not for the risk averse.

The same holds when it comes to investing. Some people can better tolerate market volatility and desire to take more risk in the hopes of a larger return. Others are less tolerant, cannot handle the thought of losing money, and invest conservatively.

Financial risk tolerance is defined as the degree of variability in investment returns that an investor is willing to withstand—more simply, your willingness to accept higher risk for potentially higher returns. And even simpler, how crazy must the market get before it keeps you up at night and you scream uncle and head for the exit?

Risk tolerance questionnaires are readily available on the Internet and will be given in some form when you sit down with most advisors. You may be asked a series of questions that attempt to determine how you would react under various financial stressors. In most cases, each answer has an associated point value. When complete, add up the score and, depending on the total, you have your risk tolerance.

There's only one - well, actually, there are many - problems with this. There is no quantifiable measure of risk tolerance - there is no score. It is a subjective measure of how you feel. It cannot be measured. Having a risk score of 50 out of 100 would be interpreted by many as having a moderate risk tolerance. But what if, for example, the questionnaire had 10 questions and you answered 5 very aggressively and 5 very conservatively? Sure, that would average to moderate, but is that the whole story?

I look at the subject much differently. The risk profile questionnaire is a document for discussion.

It's probably a discussion that will never occur if your advisor is simply attempting to sell you his product. What's far more important than ending the conversation with some fictitious score is analyzing the answers for possible contradictions. These contradictions in the way that you feel about certain risk items can create financial problems in the future.

For example, how does your expectation for a reasonable rate of return compare to asking what you would desire for a model portfolio, where your model portfolio is the percentage of high-, medium-, and low-risk investments. I've seen many instances when someone would have a target or goal of a 9 percent annual return but desire a portfolio consisting of 20 percent high risk, 40 percent medium risk, and 40 percent low risk. The two answers are contradictory and must be addressed. What if you had a moderate risk tolerance, but you were expecting a 10 percent return on your investments? Do you think that's a problem?

While simply getting an answer is all that's required by regulation, and as far as most advisors will or can go, risk tolerance is just a subjective measure that answers the question of how much risk you can psychologically handle. Simply investing in instruments that appeal to your risk tolerance may feel good or comfortable today but may have devastating long-term effects.

In addition to understanding your risk tolerance, there are two more components of your risk profile that you must understand. First, how much risk can you safely take? This is your *risk capacity*. Second, how much risk do you need? This is your *risk required*. Both risk capacity and risk required are objective, quantifiable measures.

Your risk capacity considers items such as time horizon (i.e., how long until retirement or major purchase), liquidity, wealth, income, etc., in determining the amount of risk you can safely take. For example, someone who has high income and wealth will most likely have a high- risk capacity since they should have the income streams necessary to weather short-term market downturns. Conversely, a couple living paycheck-to-paycheck, with little savings, would have a very low-risk capacity. If they had their savings in high-risk investments, a market downturn would be disastrous.

It should be apparent how ignoring risk capacity and simply investing based on your risk tolerance can create problems, especially when the two are not in agreement.

Let's look at the case of a 22-year-old, recent college graduate, who just got his first job and is enrolling in his company's 401(k). When he gets to the risk tolerance question, he remembers the havoc that the financial crisis caused his family. He wants no part of that market stress, so he states that he is conservative and invests his money in a stable value fund. Since he has approximately 45 years until he will need the money, he has a large risk capacity and can certainly risk the ups and downs of the market. If the disconnect between risk tolerance and risk capacity is not resolved, his investments will most likely yield far less than what he will need for retirement and may have trouble even keeping up with inflation.

Then there's the 65-year-old couple that is planning on retiring next year. Their money is all invested in the stock market.

They will require a large sum of money next year to purchase a home in Florida, where they will live part of the year. Their risk tolerance, as shown by their portfolio, is extremely high. Their risk capacity is much lower. They have a very short time horizon until both retirement and the need to use a large chunk of money to purchase the house. A significant downturn in the market could severely affect their plans.

Any disconnect between risk tolerance and risk capacity has the potential to cause major financial problems. Unfortunately, many people and advisors look no further than risk tolerance when they are designing the asset allocation for a portfolio.

In the case of the 22-year-old, while he could choose conservative investments where the risk in the portfolio would be at a feel-good level, this would not be prudent. His risk of not having enough money for retirement would be greatly increased.

The final part of your risk profile is your risk required. This is how much risk you need to take to achieve your financial goal. Let's look at an extremely simplistic example. I'll get into much more detail later. Assume you are retiring in 10 years and you'll need $1 million to fund your retirement plan. You currently have $500,000 and will save no more money between now and retirement. How much risk do you require to achieve your goal?

A quick calculation tells me that an average annual return of 7.2 percent will grow your account to the required $1 million, without further investment, in 10 years. The $500,000 would need to be invested in a portfolio that has an expected return of 7.2 percent annually.

The importance of knowing your risk required cannot be underestimated as it will dictate the investments and allocation required in the portfolio. Would your portfolio be invested any differently if the risk required was only 4 percent? Conversely, what would you do if the answer was a seemingly unachievable 15 percent?

Once again, just relying on your risk tolerance could create major issues. What happens when your risk required is in opposition to your risk tolerance? What if your financial plan tells you that you have a risk required of 8 percent and your risk capacity is high, but you're scared of losing money? Not so uncommon. Do you do what feels good today, or do you do what needs to be done? I never hear Suzie or Dave talk about this. Remember, I'm a risk manager.

Properly understanding your risk profile involves much more than just checking a box to designate your risk tolerance. Too often, that will be the sole basis for determining your asset allocation. How many of you are in a mutual fund or managed account that is based on your risk tolerance? This simplistic approach, while certainly compliant and safe from the brokerage or advisor's point of view, can leave you in a position of not achieving your long-term goals.

There is one more point to be made regarding risk tolerance. During periods of extreme market action (think dot-com boom and bust and the financial crisis of 2008-2009), news reports often appear that conclude that an investor's risk tolerance changes due to what is going on in the market. The assumption is that we become more risk tolerant in bull markets and more risk averse during sell-offs. The casual observer might think this was a reasonable conclusion. It's not.

While someone's risk tolerance may change over the course of their lifetime, it does not change due to short-term market action. What changes is their perception of the risk in the market.

During the dot-com boom, as the market made new highs every day, the financial media concocted the notion that there was no risk in the new companies. As I previously discussed, the market cheerleaders insisted that this was a New Economy where the rules of risk and reward were changed forever. Many investors, who would never have invested in these types of stocks, entered the market because the perception - thanks to the media—was that there was very little risk. The perceived risk fit with their more conservative risk tolerance.

Similarly, during the depths of the financial crisis in early 2009, the media was all doom and gloom. They were predicting a financial Armageddon that could take decades to recover. This was the new normal investors would need to get used to for years to come. While that was certainly a scary time, the perception of the much higher long-term risk to investors drove many out of the market, at the very worst time.

In both cases, risk tolerance stayed the same. It was the perception of risk, thanks to the financial experts, that changed.

Not convinced? A great analogy that is often used to illustrate the difference comes from the world of auto racing. I think we can all agree that race car drivers must have a pretty big appetite for risk.

A driver's tolerance for risk remains constant throughout the race; however, his perception of the risk changes constantly. He can fly down a straightaway at 200 mph because the perceived risk is low. As he approaches a sharp curve, his perception of the immediate risk increases. He cannot round the curve at 200 mph, so he slows to a point where he can negotiate the curve. His risk tolerance didn't change; his perception of the risk changed.

Why is this an important distinction? Because, as I have previously shown, individual investors tend to make decisions based on emotional factors. Changing perceptions, many caused by outside factors such as the media, can force investors into an emotional state where they make irrational decisions. Irrational decisions are bad.

The Universe of Risk

Most discussions on risk, as well as the regulations that cover advisors and most product sales, begin and end with market risk. That's a shame because there's an entire universe of risks that are just waiting to put a damper on your financial plans.

While market risk gets all the attention, its effects can be managed through a properly diversified asset allocation, which should be part of a properly constructed financial plan. There are other risks, largely ignored, that, if not accounted for, can have a disastrous impact on your plan. The most important of these are outlined below.

Inflation Risk

Inflation is the rise in prices, over time, of the goods and services we buy. How much more does your bag of groceries cost today than it did 10 or 20 years ago? How much more will it cost over the next 10 or 20 years?

During your working years, the effects of inflation are somewhat dampened by increases in wages. In retirement, when income is often fixed, the effects can be staggering. Simply illustrated, if your expenses in your first year of retirement are $60,000, at just a 3 percent inflation rate, those same expenses would cost over $80,500 in 10 years. This may be an underestimation as high-ticket items such as healthcare increase at a much higher rate. What will the inflation effect be over the course of a retirement that could last 30 years or more?

Conversely, inflation risk is also referred to as Purchasing Power Risk, as the effect of inflation will erode the purchasing power of your assets. For example, let's assume you have a $200,000 fixed-income portfolio and inflation is 3 percent. The portfolio currently yields 5 percent, which produces an income of $10,000 per year. Because of inflation, the same $10,000 would only have a purchasing power of $9,700 in year two and approximately $9,400 in year three. In 10 years, the purchasing power of the same portfolio would be reduced to less than $7,400!

Inflation risk is one of the reasons why blindly creating a portfolio based on someone's risk tolerance is dangerous. While their portfolio may be safer from the perspective of the market, a loss equal to the inflation rate - and probably a bit more - has been unknowingly built into their plan. Over time, this will necessitate the drawdown of principal in the portfolio to achieve the same purchasing power, as inflation takes hold, possibly leading to the depletion of the portfolio altogether.

When planning, it is imperative that reasonable (conservative - meaning higher) values are used for inflation estimates. Current levels of inflation are low from a historical perspective. This will not last forever. Using rates of inflation that are too low will lead to an underestimation of your needs later in life, when you may not have the income sources to make up the shortfall. A good starting point for analysis would be 3 percent to 3.5 percent, which is in line with the long-term historical average.

While market risk is on everyone's mind, inflation is insidious. Its effects take hold over years as it slowly goes about eroding your assets' ability to pay your bills.

Longevity Risk

Last time I checked, none of us were born with an expiration date stamped on the back of our necks. If we were, my job would be easy. The fact is, you don't know how long you'll live, which means there's no way to know how long you will need to fund retirement. As Americans live longer, healthier lives, the risk of outliving your money grows dramatically.

Many online resources and advisors resort to using life expectancy statistics to estimate the end date of your retirement. This date will then be used for the creation of a financial plan and investment strategy. Usually, the presentation of the plan will sound something like this: *Mr. and Mrs. Jones, using our rigorous analysis, I have designed a plan for your retirement that is designed to give you a 90 percent probability of success through life expectancy.* Sounds good, right? Not so quick. If there's one thing most people are worse at than math, it's probability.

What would happen if the advisor instead explained it this way: *Mr. and Mrs. Jones, the plan I have designed for your retirement has a less than 100 percent chance of success, and I have only run it through an age, that, by definition, you have a 50 percent chance of living past. Doesn't quite have the same appeal, does it?*

Longevity risk, outliving your money, is a serious problem and major concern for retirees. As I will show later, planning to eliminate longevity risk takes an approach not understood by the individual and rarely practiced by advisors who only want to sell products.

Sequence of Returns Risk

Once you're retired, the focus is shifted from accumulation of assets to distribution as you start to take money from your investments. You need to create a stream of income, so you can pay your bills. This is your retirement paycheck. One of the ways to create a stream of income in retirement is to take *systematic withdrawals* from your portfolio. Under this scenario, each month, an amount of your portfolio is sold to create the income you require. Usually, a larger amount is sold to account for taxes. This usually occurs each month, regardless of what's going on in the market. You need to pay the bills.

Sequence of Returns risk refers to the order in which good and bad market returns occur once you start withdrawing money from your portfolio. Most planning is done based on the average expected returns for your portfolio. Let's say you're expecting an annual return of 7 percent. It would seem reasonable that you would be able to take a 5 percent withdrawal from the portfolio annually without the risk of running out of money. Unfortunately, market returns do not occur in averages. The sequence of the returns can cause two families that have the same assets and withdrawal plans, but retire at different times, to have dramatically different outcomes.

Exhibit 6.1 Example of Sequence of Returns

| | Mr. & Mrs. Badtimer
Retired: January 2000 | | | | Mr. & Mrs. Goodtimer
Retired: January 1995 | | |
| | | | *Bothfamili.es: Beginning Balance:*
$500,000 Annual withdrawal: $25,000 | | | | |
Age	**Year**	**Return**	**Year-end Balance**		**Year**	**Return**	**Year-end Balance**
65	2000	-9.11%	$429,450		1995	38.02%	$665,100
66	2001	-11.98%	$352,152		1996	23.06%	$792,772
67	2002	-22.27%	$247,154		1997	33.67%	$1,033,253
68	2003	28.72%	$291,137		1998	28.73%	$1,303,053
69	2004	10.82%	$295,019		1999	21.11%	$1,550,668
70	2005	4.79%	$280,784		2000	-9.11%	$1,381,339
71	2006	15.74%	$295,650		2001	-11.98%	$1,186,837
72	2007	5.46%	$281,523		2002	-22.27%	$892,698
73	2008	-37.22%	$145,594		2003	28.72%	$1,118,774
74	2009	27.11%	$152,734		2004	10.82%	$1,208,821
75	2010	14.87%	$143,219		2005	4.79%	$1,234,882
76	2011	2.07%	$113,442		2006	15.74%	$1,396,328
77	2012	15.88%	$97,699		2007	5.46%	$1,438,590
78	2013	32.43%	$94,917		2008	-37.22%	$868,183
79	2014	13.81%	$73,076		2009	27.11%	$1,067,256
80	2015	1.31%	$38,526		2010	14.87%	$1,189,782
81	2016	11.92%	$7,567		2011	2.07%	$1,177,656
82	2017	**Account Exhausted**			2012	15.88%	$1,326,774

Exhibit 6.1 illustrates this point. Both families retired at age 65 with a portfolio of $500,000. Both planned to take withdrawals of $25,000 each year and increase the withdrawal annually, based on the inflation rate of the previous year.

For illustrative purposes only, I used the returns of the S&P 500 and actual inflation data. The only difference between the two families is the retirement date. Mr. and Mrs. Badtimer retired in January 2000, and Mr. and Mrs. Goodtimer retired five years earlier in January 1995.

Mr. and Mrs. Goodtimer had the good fortune of retiring at the beginning of the dot-com boom and enjoyed very positive returns in the first five years of retirement. Even after enduring the dot-com bust and the financial crisis, their account balance has grown to over $1.3 million! They should be able to live out their retirement without the fear of running out of money.

Unfortunately, the Badtimer's timing was bad. They retired just as the dot-com boom was turning to bust. Their portfolio sustained significant losses in their first three years of retirement. This caused their portfolio to be drawn down at an accelerated pace. The financial crisis of 2008 was the final nail in their portfolio's coffin. Their portfolio was at an unsustainably low level given the amount they needed to withdraw. They ran out of money at only 82 years old. Remember Bob and Joan? They retired in late 1999!

Once you reach retirement and begin to take regular withdrawals from your portfolio, the sequence of returns will matter. Flat or down markets, combined with withdrawals, in the first five years, can have a devastating long-term effect on the balance in your portfolio. Running out of money is a distinct possibility.

Systematic withdrawal strategies are favorites of the stock guys for obvious reasons. They get to keep your money. Be careful. They will use historical data and past performance to advocate for a *safe withdrawal rate* that won't deplete your account.

Relying on systematic withdrawals as your only source of retirement income creates unnecessary risk and is dangerous. As I will show later, portfolio withdrawals will be just one piece of the income you will generate in retirement. Income from other sources - *that can't run out* - will be created to help you achieve your retirement goals. After all, once your portfolio runs dry, without other sources of income, your only income may be Social Security, which probably won't be enough to meet your needs.

Elsewhere in the Universe of Risk...

Inflation, longevity, and sequence of returns are risks that should be considered in every financial plan. You need to make sure that you, or your advisor, are not using outdated rules of thumb and questionable statistics and probabilities to calculate your financial needs. These shortcuts seldom produce answers that are close to reality. By the time you realize they're wrong, it may be too late.

In my role as the risk manager for the families I work with, my philosophy is to ensure that the risks that can be controlled are controlled, even if you don't know they exist. Among these risks is a category I refer to as *Behavioral Planning Risk.*

Simply put, behavioral planning risks are those items that are preventable and can be addressed by simply trusting the planning process. Exhibit 6.2 outlines a few of the more obvious behavioral planning risks faced by most individuals.

The difference between this category of risk and most others is that behavioral planning risks are all preventable. They are caused by either inaction in an area or task or an inadvisable action.

A word of caution: investing too high a percentage of your portfolio in any single investment can create many issues, as discussed previously. Concentration Risk also opens a portal to an entirely different quadrant of the Universe of Risk where you are now exposed to all the risks that may befall a company. While going into them at this point is outside the scope of this book, think Enron, WorldCom, Lucent, and so many others. Get it?

The final category of risk you need to be aware of is that of *Event Risk.* These are all the events - mostly unwelcome - that can occur in your life that will, most likely, have an adverse financial effect. While some of these risks can be accounted

Exhibit 6.2   Behavioral Planning Risk

Procrastination Risk	Yea, we're all busy. Get it done.
Certainty of Outcome Risk	Not planning because you're sure that you're either fine or you're sure you'll never retire
Bad Assumptions Risk	Using assumptions for inflation, returns, expenses, etc., that over-estimate for assets or underestimate your expenses
Rule of Thumb Risk	Shortcuts are never a good idea. They exist to sell you something.
Shiny Object Risk	Always buying the next big investment product.
Bobblehead Risk	Not asking questions or understanding your plan
Lack of Review Risk	Even the best plans will change. You must review at least annually
Concentration risk	Too much invested in a single investment

for in the planning process by simply insuring against them, you can't insure against everything. Exhibit 6.3 outlines some of the possible event risks you may face.

The main problem with event risk is that you may never see the event coming until it happens. This makes event risk very difficult, but not impossible, to manage.

Managing these types of risk most often requires a team approach. Depending on the issue, I work closely with the lawyers, estate attorneys, accountants, and other professionals needed to create the necessary solution required for the family. Beware of the advisor who attempts to solve complex issues on their own. These complex issues almost always require the team approach to develop the correct solution.

Exhibit 6.3   Examples of Event Risk

Governmental	Life Expectancy	Health	Legal	Financial
Change in Tax Laws	Husband or Wife Die Prematurely	Husband or Wife Become Disabled	Divorce	Change or Loss of Job
Change in Social Security	Common Disaster	Husband or Wife Need Long-Term Care	Creditor Problems	Inheritance
Change in Medicare	Husband or Wife Live to Life Expectancy	Husband or Wife Need Have Chronic Illness	Legal Problems	Increase in Household Income
Change in Estate Laws	Husband Or Wife Live Past Life Expectancy	Child or Grandchild Disabled or Special Needs	Business Problems	Household Income Shrinks Dramatically
Change in Other laws	Live Way Past Life Expectancy	Care for Parent	Personal Liability	Bankruptcy

One Bad Day

My primary objective, in my role as a risk manager, is to protect the family financially against that one bad day. That's the day when the absolute worst happens. Take another look at the event risk chart, and you'll understand.

Bad things happen all the time. My job is to make sure that when bad things happen, they are not allowed to derail the long-term plans of the family because they were unaware or unprepared financially. Bad things that occur today should never be allowed to compound themselves into problems that affect tomorrow.

Hopefully, you can see that the subject of risk goes well beyond simply checking a box on a risk-tolerance question-naire or account application. While I have attempted in this chapter to outline the major sources of risk that individuals need to manage, I have only scratched the surface. As I have stated, your situation is unique. You will most likely need to manage risks that your neighbor does not. This is one more reason why generic celebrity advice is dangerous.

PART II

Planning for a Successful Retirement

CHAPTER 7

Decoding the Financial Planning Process

I cannot overstate the importance of comprehensive financial planning. As businessman and author Harvey MacKay said, *"A dream is just a dream. A goal is a dream with a plan and a deadline."* You can hope for the best, or you can plan for it. The choice is yours.

While much of what I have written so far has implications throughout every phase of your life, it's time to focus on the main theme of this book, your retirement. In retirement, unless you hit the lottery or receive a large inheritance, there are no second chances. You need to get it right the first time. This fact alone should put the importance of the planning process in perspective. Do you really want to wing it?

Unfortunately, just acknowledging the desire to create a financial plan is the easy part. Figuring out how to get it done may not be so simple. Remember, there is no generally accepted definition of financial planning. There is also no generally accepted method for constructing a financial plan. Each advisor will have their way of doing things. The process and methods used by some advisors can be a tremendous help for you and your family, while for other advisors, the financial planning process is nothing more than an elaborate show, a sales tool, designed to steer you into purchasing whatever product they want to sell.

So, how are you supposed to know what methodology is right for you? How are you supposed to tell if the advisor you're working with is helping you create a plan to achieve your future goals or just giving you a slick presentation, spit out of some selling system, designed to do nothing more than sell you a product or service? Financial planning should never be about selling. In fact, it has nothing to do with financial products. Unfortunately, you're on your own here. Remember, no regulatory authority regulates financial planning!

The financial planning process can be confusing. Many advisors - intentionally or unintentionally - will hit you with quick talking, buzzwords, and financial speak throughout the process. To make matters worse, unless you're the engineering type, math probably makes your head hurt. When confronted with a bunch of calculations, spreadsheets, charts, and graphs, you just want the madness to stop. Your inner bobblehead will keep shaking, regardless of what's being said, until the subject changes to something less painful. As important as this stuff is, most people, for various reasons, don't want to deal with the details. You want answers. The process does not need to be that difficult. There is no calculus here.

Success will come from some preparation on your part and gaining the knowledge to drive the process toward the result you desire. You need and deserve a comprehensive financial plan. Unfortunately, the financial services industry hasn't made the process easy. Not to worry, I've got your back.

Focusing on Your Retirement

Let me get something out of the way up front. At the risk of flogging the deceased equine, there are a lot of guys in this business who are only out to sell you a product. I think I may have mentioned that a few times! Some of their sales systems are extremely good at convincing you that their product is your golden ticket. The planning process must be about you and your retirement. If the conversation is all about financial products, run. You're entering the sales zone. **Remember, a product or portfolio is not a financial plan.**

Here's the red flag. If the advisor you're talking with is only licensed in one area - the securities guy or the insurance guy - then there's a very good chance their advice, and your plan, will be focused only on closing a sale. There are exceptions, but not many.

The key to getting the financial advice and plan you need is to go into the process prepared. Think of it like buying a new car. The more prepared you are, the more you've done your homework, the less the possibility that you'll walk out of the dealer with a much more expensive car containing all the upsells like extended warranties, undercoating, fabric protection, window etching, and a pair of fuzzy dice.

Financial planning is about getting the answers to the financial questions you have. For some, it will be finding the answers to the financial issues that are keeping them up at night and affecting their life. For others, planning will be about turning a lifetime of work and saving into the retirement of their dreams. This process is about you and your family—not the advisor, their practice, or the products they're selling. You must make sure that you are the focus. You need to drive the process.

Preparing for a successful financial planning experience must begin before sitting down with an advisor. The first step must be an honest conversation with your spouse, partner, or the person you plan on growing old with, about your goals, dreams, and how you want to spend your retirement. If you're flying solo, you'll still need to go through this process.

This discussion may be the most important part of the planning process and the one that seldom occurs. When I sit down with a family to discuss their retirement plan, the first topic we discuss is their goals. I'm amazed that most couples have never had a conversation about what they want to do when they retire. When the subject comes up in the meeting, there's usually just an awkward pause where we all stare at each other. The sound of crickets is all that can be heard!

I will usually force the conversation, even if I must have it with each person separately. It's that important. When I finally get the couple to open up about what they want, it can turn into a pretty emotional conversation. Often, the couple was never aware of each other's dreams for retirement. I will get deeper into the conversation in the next chapter.

If you are going through the process of planning for your future, wouldn't it be a good thing to plan for the future you want? Now is the time. Regardless of whether you feel your goals are achievable or not, this is the time to have the conversation. Planning alone will not guarantee that you can achieve all your retirement goals or that all your dreams will come true. However, I've worked with many families that were surprised at what they were able to achieve with the proper planning and a little time. Whether it's travel, a beach house, restoring a classic car from your youth, or anything else, you may never know what's within your reach if you don't include it in the conversation today.

A word of caution: Very often, there is one spouse that will defer to the other during the planning process. They assume that because their spouse has handled all the financial issues to this point, that retirement planning is no different. This decision may stem from the belief that planning is simply an investment discussion. Do not let this happen. You must include both of your hopes, dreams, and desires in the planning process. It is vitally important.

Once you've established your priorities for your financial plan, keeping the process on track will be much easier. If the advisor is not addressing your priorities, it may be time to find a new advisor.

The Phases of Retirement Planning

While they may be used interchangeably, saving for retirement is very different from planning for retirement. When you are in your 20s, 30s, and even most of your 40s, your focus should be on simply developing the saving and investing habits that will allow you to begin to build your retirement nest egg. At these ages, there are most likely many other items that will be competing for your dollars and should be the focus of your financial planning. Purchasing a house, college for the kids, etc., will be where the bulk of your dollars are going. At this point, creating the savings habits in retirement and non-retirement accounts, along with a sound investment strategy, will be your best plan to prepare for the years ahead.

With regard to your retirement, this is referred to as the *accumulation phase.* During the accumulation phase, the focus is on saving or accumulating assets for retirement. Formal retirement planning during this time is of little value as the time to retirement and the number of unknowns is just too great.

Most advisors subscribe to a two-phase retirement model. Under this scenario, the accumulation phase begins the day you start saving for retirement and ends on the day before retirement begins. On the day you retire, you are immediately thrust into the *distribution phase.* Here, your accumulated assets - the money you saved for retirement - will be distributed - or spent—to fund your retirement income. This view of retirement is a very simplistic view of the process that is presented by many advisors. Your inner bobblehead will be nodding along when it is explained to you as it seems to make sense.

The problem with this picture of the retirement planning process is that it makes the implied assumption that the assets you used to accumulate your nest egg will be the same ones you use to derive your retirement income. This is a dangerous assumption as most of your money may be in the market. Remember, relying on systematic withdrawals from your investment accounts as your only source of retirement income creates sequence of returns and longevity risk problems. First, we manage risk.

The two-phase model of retirement planning also implies that the change from accumulation to distribution happens at a point in time, the day you retire. While most sane people would understand that they need to address retirement issues before the day they retire, this model tends to de-emphasize the importance and magnitude of the work that must be done to ensure retirement success.

I employ a three-phase model for retirement preparation which emphasizes the need for planning well before the date of retirement. In addition to the accumulation and distribution phases, a third phase, the *transition phase,* is added in between. The transition phase, as the name implies, is where you shift your focus from accumulation to distribution, from working to retirement. It's silly to think that these will be accomplished in a single day, as the two-phase model implies.

The transition phase ideally begins *at least* 10 to 15 years before your target retirement date and is where you will begin detailed retirement planning in earnest. Adding the transition phase to the retirement planning model emphasizes the need and timeframe for planning, as well as repositioning your assets from emphasizing capital appreciation to being able to generate the income you'll need in retirement. I'll get much deeper into the transition phase in later chapters. For now, beware of the advisor that oversimplifies the planning process.

What's Your Number?

Perhaps you remember the ING commercial where everyone is walking around holding a number? That number, as the commercial pointed out, was, according to some software, the amount of money you would need for retirement.

That premise, at first glance, has some appeal. If you could easily calculate the amount of money you would need to have a financially successful retirement, it should then be a simple matter to come up with a plan to save that amount by the day you want to retire, whether that was next year or 20 years from now. It seems to make sense, or does it?

If you recall from Chapter 1, the rules of retirement have changed. The demise of the traditional pension and the rise of self-directed retirement plans have led to a change in the way we think about our retirement savings and planning. Instead of thinking in terms of income, as we do with a pension and Social Security, the focus, and obsession, is on your investment account balance. I refer to this as the *big number/small number* debate, where the big number represents your account balances, and the small number represents the monthly income you'll require in retirement.

During your working years, things are relatively simple. You work, you get paid. Each month, most of you have a good idea how much income you'll receive. You receive a paycheck that, unless you're on commission, doesn't change much. This paycheck is your income.

The biggest difference between your last day of work and your first day of retirement is the fact that you will no longer receive a paycheck. Your entire adult life is based off that paycheck. It determines the house you live in, the car you drive, and where you go on vacation. Why should things be any different in retirement? You still need a paycheck, don't you?

Your transition to retirement should not include having to figure out the logistics of how to pay your bills every month. Your objective in planning must be to create a monthly cash flow which is sufficient to meet your retirement income needs.

As you enter the planning process, it is imperative that you understand the result of the planning you'll be doing and whether the focus will be on the big or small number. What's your objective? Is it to create a plan that simply gives you a big number in retirement? Or is it to satisfy the goal we agreed to earlier? To create a plan where on the first day and every day of retirement, you will have the money to pay your bills and that you can never, ever, under any circumstance run out of money, regardless of what happens in the market, the economy, the world, or politics? Having a big number is no plan. Having a big balance in your brokerage account with no idea how to turn it into the income you will need to last throughout your retirement will never assure you of having enough money to make it through retirement. Just ask Bob and Joan.

The result of your planning should be your complete road-map to, and through, retirement. In a very simple manner, it should be able to illustrate not only your income needs but where that income will come from.

The best way to ensure you're keeping the planning process on track is to keep asking yourself, "Does this make sense?" If the answer is anything but "yes," it's time to take a step back and evaluate the process.

Building Your Plan: Which Method?

Three things will determine the value of your final plan and its ability to help you achieve your retirement goals. First, your involvement and the accuracy of the data you provide. Remember, garbage in - garbage out! Second, the knowledge and ethics of your advisor. Are they there to advise or simply to close a deal? And third, the software and methods used by you or your advisor to create your plan. Since the first is rather obvious and the second is an ongoing theme of this book and an issue I'll get back to later, let's focus on the third.

In the financial advisory world, there are two distinct methods of financial planning used by advisors: *Cash flow-based planning* and *goal-based planning.* Like so many other topics in this business, there is an ongoing battle among advisors as to which method is best, with strong feelings on both sides of the fight. While many experts continually debate the subject, the answer, as I will show, is obvious. While both methods have their uses, they are not, as many advisors may tell you, interchangeable.

Cash flow planning is a method of planning that focuses on understanding and projecting your expenses in a highly detailed manner. It operates under the premise that the biggest determinant of the success of your financial plan will be the understanding of, accounting for, and control of your expenses, both before and during retirement. Without this understanding of your expenses, even if your investments outperform the market every year, you may still experience financial shortfalls.

Here, the planning process begins with an exhaustive analysis of your current financial picture with the emphasis on your expenses. It's extremely important to get a good starting point. While it may seem like a simple exercise, very often it takes a few tries before the data is sound. A good advisor will spend the time here to ensure that the data makes sense.

The result of a cash flow-based plan is essentially a budget document that shows your periodic expenses and where the income to cover them will come from. The focus is on the small number. Cash flow planning relies less on pretty graphs and charts (although they're usually available) and more on the creation of your personal financial statements. The goal is to give you the information to see exactly how you will pay your bills each month.

Isn't this pretty much the way you handle things when you are working? Why should things be any different in retirement? The objective of your financial plan is to create a stream of cash flows that will be sufficient to fund your expenses. In other words, create a retirement paycheck. As I pointed out earlier, it's ridiculous to expect you to suddenly, on day one of your retirement, figure out where the cash to pay the bills is going to come from every month. In retirement, cash flow is king. It's the foundation upon which your retirement lifestyle is built.

Goal-based planning was developed to simplify and shorten the planning process. Advisors realized that many of their clients just wanted an easy way to understand where they stood and what to do financially, without the work and detail involved in cash flow- based planning.

Goal-based planning is much less intensive as it relies more on estimates and assumptions than cash flow-based planning. It works well for expenses that have known, or easily estimated, costs, such as funding your newborn's college education, buying a car, a house, or taking that dream vacation. The amounts can be estimated, the timeframe is usually known, and a rate of return can be assumed. Given these inputs, a saving rate can be easily calculated and tracked to check the progress of funding your goal.

Retirement is handled in the same manner as other goals. Your retirement is analyzed, in its entirety, as a goal. The software then attempts to answer the big number question: How much money will you need to retire?

Goal-based planning is an effective methodology when you are younger, and the focus is on funding specific goals. It can also be effective for getting younger clients to focus on the need to begin to save for retirement. Using the methodology for retirement purposes, however, doesn't pass the common-sense test. Does it make sense to you that you can take a few estimates and assumptions, plug them into a piece of software that makes even more estimates and assumptions, and come up with an answer that means anything? Not likely.

While there are many problems with using goal- based planning to construct a retirement plan, there is one major flaw that makes it useless. *Retirement is not a goal!* While you will certainly have goals that you want to achieve in retirement - that's the point of retirement—retirement is a phase of life that can last a long time. Think about it this way, can you attribute a big number to your current phase of life? No. You require a stream of income.

To me, the debate over whether one method is superior is nonsense. The sophistication of the software that is available to advisors makes them both valuable tools, if used properly. The question as to which method is superior will depend on your current phase of life. When you are younger, in the accumulation phase, goal-based planning is far superior to cash flow-based planning. The emphasis during this phase in on saving for specific goals. As for retirement, ballpark estimates at this point are fine. The point of planning at this stage is to make you understand that while you may have short-term goals to save for, you cannot forget about retirement. Cash flow-based planning for retirement at this point is frankly a waste of time as the length of time to retirement and the number of unknowns is simply too great to have any value.

Once you enter the transition phase - ideally, at least ten years prior to your target retirement date—and begin the retirement planning process, cash flow planning is the only answer. The detailed analysis will allow you to understand how you'll fund the cash flows - pay your bills - in retirement. Here, you must focus on the small number. Cash flow planning treats retirement as a continuation of life, not a single goal.

The answer as to which method is superior seems to be obvious. So why all the fuss? The reality is that software to build these plans is expensive and can have a very steep and long learning curve. It can take a lot of training and a good amount of time to get to the point that an advisor can effectively use these systems to create financial plans for their clients. Because of this, many advisors I speak with will only commit to one method. Instead of being honest about their limitation, they would rather act like a bunch of six year olds yelling about how their way is best. That shouldn't be your problem. If you are in the transition phase, regardless of the story your guy may give you, if they are using a goal-based system for your retirement plan, you need to find another advisor.

Beware the Black Box

There is a third method of planning for retirement that you must stay away from at all costs. In this digital, do-it-yourself, self-directed, retirement world, many people are using the online retirement calculators to answer their retirement questions. Less qualified advisors are using similar tools to give quick answers to clients, often as a simple way to close a sale.

Offered on the websites of practically every brokerage, financial institution, media outlet, and other sites that have nothing to do with finance or retirement, these calculators purport to be able to tell you your retirement needs, from as few as four pieces of data.

Even though the very premise that these calculators operate under is beyond ridiculous, I have met many people who have used them as the basis of their financial planning. Much like the TV financial personalities, these sites are also full of disclosures and disclaimers (in very fine print) that warn the users that the results are for educational purposes and should not be taken as personal advice. These disclaimers are usually ignored, if they are read at all.

Just like the gurus that are paraded out in the financial media, it is the implied authority of many of these sites that get people to believe they are getting accurate information, instead of, in the case of the brokerages and financial companies, a veiled attempt to get you to give them a call.

How bad are these calculators? To illustrate, I conducted a test using ten online retirement calculators from well-known and reputable sources from the financial services industry, media, advocacy, and even a regulatory organization. The ten calculators used were from the websites of AARP, Bankrate. com, CNNMoney, Edward Jones, Fidelity, FINRA (the self-regulatory body of the securities industry), Schwab, T. Rowe Price, Vanguard, and Voya.

I conducted the test using a fictitious 50-year-old married couple planning to retire at the age of 70. The couple has a combined income of $200,000 and has saved $350,000 for retirement. They are currently saving 10 percent of their income each year. Their goal is to have a retirement income that lets them spend at their pre-retirement level.

Each calculator required a different number of inputs from the user and used default estimates for the rest. I was astounded at how little data some of the sites required to give a result.

The calculators gave results in one of two different ways. They either showed the big number they projected the couple was on-track to have at retirement, and the big number they would need for retirement, or the calculator's idea of the small number of monthly income the couple was on-track to have, and the income they would need.

The results among the different calculators were wildly different. Six of the ten sites purported to calculate the amount of money the couple would need for their entire retirement - the big number. According to the data, the couple would need between $2,451,024 and $5,000,000 to retire. They were on track to have between $1,589,973 and $2,300,000 saved at the time they retire. The shortfall estimated for the couple ranged from $432,230 to $2,700,000!

The results from the four sites that calculated the monthly income amount - the small number - were no better. The monthly income needed ranged from $11,666 to $14,167, while the projected income available ranged from $5,306 to $10,263. The income shortfall ranged from $2,607 to $6,547 per month. That's $31,284 to $78,564 per year!

There is absolutely no way, by using this methodology, to determine if any of the results are anywhere close to accurate, as most of the calculators had major flaws in logic. Only two of the ten calculators distinguished between married and single. This omission led to obvious issues with the Social Security results. Current and future savings and investments were not segregated between taxable, nontaxable, and tax-deferred accounts, creating potentially large differences in the tax liability during retirement, one of the largest factors from an income perspective and one that the calculators and many goal-based systems often ignore. There were too many other issues with the methodologies to go into. The point is moot. In short, each calculator used a different algorithm and different assumptions for figuring out your answer.

My point here is to illustrate the variability, uselessness, and danger of relying on results using this type of methodology. Relying on simple tools is about as useful and financially dangerous as tuning in to CNBC at a random time and acting on the current interview's opinion on a stock.

Let's assume for a moment that using calculators or goal-based methods to create your retirement plan wasn't a really bad idea. You're 57 and, along with your advisor, you just completed your financial plan that says you'll need $1 million for retirement. Fast forward 10 years to the first day of your retirement. You've got your million. Now what? How do you live off that money? The result of your retirement planning should never leave you asking, "Now what?!"

Focusing on big numbers without a plan for how you can create income is nuts! It is easy, though. Simply plug some numbers into a calculator, use some simple rules of thumb that your quick talking advisor will use to get your bobblehead nodding, sprinkle with some wishful thinking, and congratulations, you have a plan that is almost certainly worthless and doomed to failure. Does that make much sense to you?

In my opinion, the problem with using goal-based planning for retirement is that it employs too many shortcuts. Your situation is far more complex than something that can be reduced to a series of estimates, and assumptions. Shortcuts that require little effort on your part are not likely to provide meaningful results. Remember, in retirement, there are no do-overs. You deserve better.

Once again, betting your future on the probability that a big number, calculated using questionable methods, will not run out is a needless risk to take.

What if I'm Wrong?

Regardless of the methodology used to create your retirement plan, certain estimates and assumptions will need to be made. At the very least, inflation rates, rates of return, and the future value of assets that are planned to be sold must be estimated for perhaps the next 30 years or more. Remember, no one knows what will happen in the future ... and if they did, they wouldn't tell you.

Rate assumptions will have a huge effect on the results of your plan. Some advisors, either intentionally or from lack of knowledge, may use current rates in your plan. For example, the current inflation rate (as reported by the government) is at historically low levels. In your plan, it's a mistake to assume that these rates will continue for the long term. Using too low of an inflation estimate will greatly underestimate your expenses in retirement. The same holds for using too high of a rate of return on your investments.

I prefer to use very conservative assumptions when I build a financial plan. For example, I will always use a higher rate of inflation, lower rates of return, and lower asset values. Each year that we have lower than estimated inflation, or higher than estimated returns, builds a little more cushion into the plan for the things we cannot anticipate.

Beware of the advisor that tries to use less conservative rates to develop your plan. Very often, if an advisor can show you that the plan he developed will be successful, you will happily agree with his recommendations. This could spell disaster if the market and economy don't perform just right—as they often don't.

Rules for a Retirement Plan

After the meeting with Bob and Joan, I made it my mission to ensure that what happened to them couldn't happen to you. I knew that most people who go to an advisor have no idea what to expect, the questions to ask, or even the result they should be getting. I saw this as the first area I needed to address.

Without rules to govern financial planning or the financial planning process, you are left to figure out if the advisor sitting across from you is there to help or sell. Even if the advisor does have your best interest in mind, does his process match what you require to prepare for retirement properly?

Note: Once again, please refer to the appendix of this book for a list of questions you must ask the advisor before you begin work. These questions, along with an understanding of the rules laid out below, will be your best assurance of receiving the advice you are looking for, as well as your best defense against the sales guy.

I developed the following rules after studying the planning and sales methodologies of other advisors and their companies. I've been pretty clear on what's necessary for your financial plan. If your advisor strays from these rules, they may be practicing a planning methodology that may not be what you expect.

Rule #1: The methodology must be process driven, not sales driven. The process should be about planning your future, not selling you a product. If you get that uncomfortable feeling you are about to be sold something, you probably are. Time to move on to a new advisor.

Rule #2: The process must be collaborative. It's your plan, your future. You must be actively involved in the process. The plan will be of little value if it doesn't answer your questions and address your goals.

Rule #3: The plan must be cash flow based to calculate the income you will need in retirement. You MUST plan for the small number! Regardless of the level of assets you may have accumulated over the years, without a thorough understanding of your income requirements, there is no way to ensure that those assets can produce the retirement lifestyle you want, without the risk of running out of money.

We need to look no further than the case of Bob and Joan to see the disastrous effects of not having an income plan. Also, how many stories have you heard of lottery winners or multi-million-dollar athletes who had enough money for ten lifetimes and still went bankrupt? They didn't plan for income, either.

While your level of wealth, family situation, or business considerations may require more involved planning, an income plan is always where we start. It is through this process that many of the other issues will be uncovered.

Rule #4: The plan must be easy to understand. Beware of advisors that use buzzwords and financial jargon. A plan can only be successful if you fully understand every part of the process from the creation of the plan to the execution. Most important, you MUST fully understand the financial products that are being used to fund and execute your plan. Too often, when I review the holdings of a family that was working with another advisor, they have no idea what they own, how it works, or what it's supposed to do. Education is a large part of the process. Once again, don't be a bobblehead!

Rule #5: The execution of the plan cannot be based on historical data or averages. This rule also includes rules-of-thumb, conventional wisdom, old wives' tales, etc. While some historical averages will be used in the analysis phase, such as inflation rates and rates of return, these can never be used as a basis for the execution of the plan. This will become much clearer a little later.

Always be wary when your advisor uses a *rule* as the basis for your plan. Most rules are not rules at all, but simply shortcuts that, once upon a time, may have been valid.

Rule #6: The plan cannot be based on life expectancy. As previously discussed, life expectancy is an average. You don't come with an expiration date. Neither should your retirement plan.

Rule #7: The plan must be dynamic. Over the years, there will be changes in your situation that were not part of your original plan. Whether the change is caused by some event (see event risk in chapter 6) or simply the desire to change your retirement goals, the plan needs to be easily revised for any changes that occur. The plan must also be able to run different scenarios you may want to explore. At the very least, scenarios need to be run for such things as the premature death of either spouse.

Rule #8: The plan must be trackable. The financial planning process is not a one-time event. It is an ongoing process throughout the transition phase and into and through retirement. You must be able to keep track of your progress. More on this in chapter 14.

Rule #9: The plan must be product agnostic. The success or failure of a financial plan cannot be based on specific products. That's sales, not planning. While there will be an ideal mix of products that will be recommended for the execution of your plan, no one product or class of products should be absolutely required.

Getting Started

Arming yourself with a little knowledge and the confidence to take an active role in the financial planning process will often make the difference between creating your roadmap to the retirement you desire and a piece of paper that does nothing but justify the product you just purchased. There can be no bobbleheads here. Always ask yourself if the process and results make sense. Often, looking for answers to the simple, obvious questions can be the quickest way to tell if the final product will have the value you desire.

Remember, you're not an investment manager or a cash manager, and you shouldn't need to be. It's a problem if your retirement plan is so complex that it requires you to become both on your first day of retirement. That's risky and unfair, given that the cost of failure is so high. If you're retiring with a plan that requires you to have an MBA to understand and manage, you might have the wrong plan and the wrong advisor.

It's time to get started creating your financial plan and the *Retirement Income Plan* that will show how you are going to pay for the lifestyle and goals that you've worked so hard for all these years.

CHAPTER 8

The Financial Planning Process for Retirement

The major problem with many of the financial plans I review is they are long on pretty graphs and charts and short on detail. Financial planning is an ongoing process, not a one-time event. The result of your planning efforts must be more than just a stack of paper.

Most planning usually focusses on just two points in time: the day you retire and your life expectancy. Forgetting for a moment the questionable validity of the methods used to perform the analysis, looking at just two points in time can serve no purpose in helping your transition into retirement.

Remember, your financial plan should serve as your road-map from where you are today to not only the day you retire but all the way through retirement. It should be able to show you not just where you're going, but where you are, or should be, at any point along the journey. How else can you know if you're on track?

Having a plan that only shows a midpoint (retirement) and an endpoint (life expectancy) would be like taking a trip with a map that had the place you wanted to go but contained no roads or other details. If you were driving from New Jersey to California, you'd probably want some indication you were heading in the wrong direction before you saw the *Welcome to Florida sign.* That's just not possible if your map doesn't contain the data.

Retirement will be a major change in your life. My objective is to ensure that your transition to retirement, from a financial perspective, will be as simple, comfortable, and as stress free as possible.

As I've discussed, the planning process is a bit more involved than answering a few questions and waiting for a report. While it should require some effort on your part, this shouldn't be a difficult exercise. In this chapter, I will walk you through the process I use with the families I work with, step-by-step.

Step 1: The Conversation

As I touched on in the previous chapter, the starting point for your financial planning experience must be a conversation with your spouse/partner, if you have one, to agree on your retirement goals. It is imperative that you start the process with a common destination - you must start on the same page.

Since most couples usually don't have the conversation before our first meeting, I will spend time during *Discovery* - my first meeting with a family - to go over the importance of the conversation and coach them through what they need to accomplish. This conversation must be about the specifics of how you want to live your retirement and the things you want to accomplish. It should not be a conversation about investments, market strategies, financial products, or anything else not related to your retirement goals. There will be plenty of time for those discussions later.

For simplicity and clarity, I will have the couple separate the conversation into three categories:

Intermediate goals, retirement lifestyle, and ultimate goals and desires.

Intermediate goals are the things you would like to accomplish before retirement. For example, buying a vacation home, a boat, traveling, finishing a degree, paying for your kid's wedding, etc., are all items that would fit into this category. This would also include other major expenses, such as home renovations and education for the kids. The point here is not to get wrapped up in semantics but to be able to account for all the things that you need or want to get done before retirement.

The next category covers your retirement lifestyle. We all have different ideas about how we want to live our retirement. How do you envision yours? Do you want to travel extensively or are you the type that wants to stay at home and take care of the grandkids? Different lifestyles will have different price tags attached to them.

Included in the lifestyle conversation should be a discussion about where you'll live. Are you planning on staying in your current house or perhaps downsizing? Will you stay in the area you currently live or retire to a warmer (and perhaps cheaper) state like Florida, the Carolinas, or Arizona, if you're not there already? Perhaps, if you're from the North, you plan on becoming *snowbirds* and having winter and summer homes. Residence issues may be the most important part of the conversation. They'll be a major component of your retirement lifestyle and probably have a big impact—positively or negatively—on your expenses.

There may be some overlap and timing issues between your intermediate goals and retirement lifestyle. For instance, you may plan on downsizing before retirement or purchase a vacation house that will someday become your retirement residence. Once again, do not get bogged down by worrying about categories or timing. The important point is that the two of you agree on the lifestyle for which you are planning. The more agreement you have now, the fewer issues you'll have later. There's little point in going through the exercise only to come to an end and find out that the retirement you planned for is not the retirement you had in mind.

The final part of your conversation should cover your ultimate goals and desires. These are the big goals or dreams you may have in the back of your mind. For example, I have one family that wants to buy a vineyard and produce wine and another that wants to take a six-month trip around the world. They both recognize that these are audacious dreams that may, or may not, be possible. You may have similar dreams for your retirement. While many desires may not be possible given your resources, without including them in the process, you may never know.

This conversation is undoubtedly the most important part of planning for your retirement. It will ensure that you and your spouse are both planning for the retirement you both desire. Agreement here is imperative. If you don't, or can't, agree on the retirement you want to live, perhaps a conversation with a different type of professional is in order!

Step 2: Data Collection and the Year-One Analysis

The purpose of the Year-One Analysis is to develop the first estimate of the amount of income you'll need, and the amount of assets you'll have, the year you retire. Notice I didn't say the amount of assets you will need.

That will come later. The first step in accomplishing this task is to create your current personal financial statements.

For a business, the key financial statements consist of the Profit and Loss Statement (P&L) and the Balance Sheet. The P&L reports current income and expenses, with the result being the *net income* of the business on a periodic basis. A business' balance sheet reports their assets, liabilities, and something called shareholder equity (you don't need to worry about that one). The result of the balance sheet is the *net worth* of the business.

For families, the financial statements are similar. Your P&L will track your current net cash flow, which is simply your income minus your expenses. Your balance sheet will track your net worth, which is your assets minus your debt. Don't worry; it's a lot easier than it sounds!

Your job is to provide the numbers. For the families I work with, I do the rest.

Starting with the objective of creating your personal financial statements eliminates the possibility - and the urge - to take shortcuts. This step is too important. It is the foundation upon which your entire financial plan will be built. You should run screaming from any advisor who attempts to derive your numbers using calculators and estimates based on assumptions and guesses. While this step will require a little work on your part, as you will see, it is simple and will be well worth the effort.

Let's start with your P&L. Your mission here is to account for all your current sources of income and expenses. I have families compile these numbers using a spreadsheet I will provide that contains many of the more common categories of income and expenses.

For income, your gross income will be the starting point. I will adjust for your payroll deductions, particularly any retirement or other savings deductions, and get to your net after-tax or take-home pay. Starting with the gross income allows me to capture more detail than starting with net income. This detail will be important later.

Your expenses are everything you pay on a monthly/ annual basis. The more of your expenses you can account for, the more accurate the starting point. Accuracy is sometimes difficult on the first attempt. We all have *leakage.* That's the money that mysteriously disappears from our wallets. I know for me it usually goes to fund my coffee habit! Try to account for as much as possible. Small errors will get magnified over the 10 or 20 years you may have until retirement.

The difference between your income and expenses is your net cash flow and should have some relation to the amount of money you save (or not) each month.

Next, you'll work on your personal balance sheet. This data simply consists of the current values of your assets minus the current value of your debt. Once again, I provide help in the form of a spreadsheet to assist in compiling the appropriate data.

Exhibit 8.1   Example of Personal P&L Statement

Annual Income	
Salary, Wages, Commissions	$175,000
Less: Payroll Deductions	
Social Security Tax	$10,850
Medicare Tax	$2,538
Income Tax: Federal	$22,750
Income Tax: State	$8,750
401(k) / Savings Plans	$10,500
Net Income from Salary	$119,613
Other Income	
Interest & Dividends	$3,300
Total Net Income	$122,913
Annual Expenses	
Living Expenses	
Home Expenses excl. taxes and mortgage)	$16,000
Auto & Transportation	$9,000
Daily Living (Food, Clothing, Supplies, etc.)	$9,000
Entertainment & Recreation	$8,500
Travel & Vacations	$5,000
Insurances (excluding life)	$1,500
Life Insurance	$6,000
Medical	$2,400
Property Tax	$9,000
Miscellaneous	$8,500
Debt Service	
Mortgage Payments (principal & Interest)	$19,250
Loan Payments (car, installment, student, etc.)	$9,500
Minimum Credit Card Payments	$4,000
Total Expenses	$107,650
Net Annual Cash Flow	$15,263

Usually, a balance sheet will contain the value of all assets you own. For this analysis, you will restrict the assets to only those that will have value for your retirement. For instance, you should include the value of any real estate you own, including your primary residence. You will also include the value of all investment accounts. These should be accounted for separately as you must be aware of the tax treatment of the accounts (taxable, tax-free, tax-deferred). While it will not affect the net worth calculation, it will affect income calculations later if you need to pay the tax man.

Unless an asset is to be sold as part of your retirement planning, assets such as cars, furniture, other possessions, and even collectibles will not be included in the balance sheet.

For the liabilities, the value of all debt needs to be included. These include the outstanding balance on a mortgage or home equity line, all credit card balances, student loans, personal loans, and any other debt you may have racked up.

The difference between the assets and the liabilities is your current net worth or how much money you would have if you sold your house, liquidated all your investment accounts, and paid off all your debts. Over time, we would expect this number to increase as asset values appreciate and debt is paid off.

The Year-One Analysis process is thoroughly discussed during the discovery meeting. After the meeting, if we mutually agree to proceed, I will send the necessary data collection spreadsheets to the family for completion. I ask that the data be returned before the next meeting with the family, so I have time to review. This allows time to undertake some simple logic tests and develop a list of questions for review.

Step 3: The Review Meeting

Once the family completes the data gathering for the Year-One Analysis and I've had some time to look it over, we will get together for the *Review Meeting*. The purpose of the Review Meeting is to review the data provided by the family and

Exhibit 8.2   Retirement Asset Balance Sheet

Assets	
Cash	
Savings & Money Market	$27,000
Checking Accounts	$8,000
CDs	$15,000
Investments	
Brokerage Accounts (non-retirement)	$275,000
Other Securities	$26,000
Life Insurance (cash value)	$55,000
IRAs	$165,000
Qualified Plans (401(k), 403(b) etc.)	$217,000
Annuities (surrender value)	$75,000
Real Estate	
Primary House (to be sold at retirement)	$565,000
Total Assets Available for Retirement	**$1,428,000**
Liabilities	
Mortgages	$225,000
Car Loans	$16,250
Credit Cards	$5,000
Student Loans	$12,540
Other Liabilities	$3,650
Total Liabilities	**$262,440**
Net Worth (Retirement)	**$1,165,560**

gather all the information I will need to complete the analysis and ultimately the family's financial plan.

Please note: The Review Meeting, which is usually the second time we get together, is the first time I will ask to see personal information such as account statements, tax returns, etc. I never ask the family to produce these in the Discovery

Meeting. Be very wary of the advisor that requires you to bring all your personal information to the first meeting.

The most important part of a client/advisor relationship is trust. Until I've met a family and we've mutually agreed to work together, I have not earned the right to see this information. With all the issues these days surrounding the security of personal information, does it make sense that the first thing you do when you enter the office of an advisor you probably never met is to give all your personal information to the lowest paid person in the office to copy or scan?

The first part of the Review Meeting is spent going over the information provided during the data gathering for the Year-One Analysis. My objective is to make sure I understand the numbers and ensure the inputs makes sense. I take nothing for granted. The accuracy (or lack thereof) of your numbers will flow through every other part of your plan. It's extremely important that you have an accurate starting point. Any time a number is produced, you always need to ask if it makes sense. Mistakes happen. These can be either in logic or input. Doing a little sanity check will ensure that both the inputs and output have a basis in reality.

To ensure accuracy, during my review with the family, I will do some quick logic checks to determine if the initial numbers make sense. First, I will compare the reported total monthly expenses to the total monthly net (take home) income. Is there a surplus or a deficit? Does this make sense to the family?

The second logic check I will undertake is to review discretionary expenses. Is there an entry for items such as entertainment, vacations, dining out, etc.? If included, do the amounts make sense? Discretionary expenses are often knowingly - or unknowingly - left out of the analysis.

I will never take a number for granted and assume its validity. Neither should you. I will continue to ask questions and refine the data for both your P&L and Balance Sheet until we are all satisfied that the data is as accurate as possible.

Having a solid starting point is paramount in producing meaningful results.

Believe it or not, that was the hard part. Once this data is locked down, it's time to continue toward year one.

The second part of the Review Meeting is dedicated to the results of your retirement goal conversation. Do you agree on your goals and the lifestyle you want to live in retirement? If so, we can proceed.

The objective here is to take the results of the conversation and attach timing and cost to each one. Having goals is fine, but eventually, if they are to become a reality, you'll need the cash flow to pay for them.

We start with the intermediate goals and expenses as some of them may be fast approaching. For each item, you need to estimate the year the expense will occur and the cost per year, in today's dollars. The timing on some of these items, such as paying for your kid's college education, may be well known. Others may be more of a guess, such as paying for your daughter's wedding. Still others may be more of a wish, like buying that boat you've had your eye on, sometime in the next five years.

We estimate the cost of these items in current dollars for two reasons. First, it should be easy to get the price of something today. Whether it's a boat or college tuition, the current price should be easy to find. Second, since the date of the expense may move from the original projection, the estimated cost will most likely change due to inflation. If current costs are used as a baseline, calculating a new cost based on a change in timing is a simple mathematical equation.

The same exercise is undertaken for your lifestyle goals. While the timing of many of these events will be unknown and possibly change many times before they occur, our objective for this exercise is to establish a baseline or starting point. Remember, your financial plan is not a static document. It cannot be allowed to gather dust or get lost in a file. It is designed to be periodically reviewed and updated as your situation, and possibly your goals, change. More on that later.

The next part of the Review Meeting is to uncover the changes to your cash flow that will occur between today and your retirement. For example, what are the savings that are realized when your children graduate and move out on their own? Reductions in expenses from items such as cell phones, car insurance, groceries, and clothes can be significant. Items such as paying off your house or other debt will be gathered during the review of your balance sheet data.

The final part of the Review Meeting will be spent discussing your ultimate goals for retirement. Many people, I find, never discuss these retirement dreams because they see no way that they will ever be able to accomplish them. This may very well be the case. However, once a financial plan is established that will allow a family to achieve the retirement lifestyle they desire, why not see if some of these dreams can be made a reality? Often, the only thing that prevents a dream from becoming a reality is having the desire to plan for it.

The Review Meeting may raise other questions that must be answered or require other data to be compiled. Once all the data has been compiled and checked, the analysis can begin.

Step 4: The Analysis

Now that we have a good understanding of your current cash flow and the cost and timing of your intermediate and lifestyle goals, I can get to work and complete the Year-One Analysis.

To calculate the amount of income you will need year one of retirement, your small number, and the value of your saving and investments, your big number, your P&L and balance sheet simply need to be projected out to your first year of retirement. Simply? How can this be done with any degree of accuracy when retirement might be ten, fifteen, or more years into the future?

Once you have a solid starting point, the difference between your cash flow today and at any point in the future is simply a matter of accounting for inflation and the changes to cash flow and your intermediate goals, which you compiled in the Review Meeting.

Your current assets and investments will be projected forward using conservative rates of return appropriate for each asset. The balances will be adjusted each year for additional savings or investments, such as your annual IRA or 401(k) contributions.

At this point, it is worth noting that while it is possible to complete the analysis using a spreadsheet program, I use financial planning software that has been specifically designed for this analysis. This both increases accuracy by eliminating common spreadsheet errors and gives the ability to stress test the results by testing various assumptions. Using the software also allows revisions to the analysis to be done very simply, making your ultimate plan much easier to complete, less time consuming, and far more accurate.

Detail is important here. While it would be easy to put all the data into the planning software and spit out a single number for your income needs, this is of little value. The point of the analysis, once again, is a starting point that will be reviewed and updated periodically. The more detail there is, the more I can account for changes.

Because inflation is one of the biggest risks to the success of your financial plan over the course of a long retirement, we must ensure that it is accounted for properly. Not all expenses will be subject to inflation at the same rate. Items such as healthcare and education have historically been subject to much higher rates of inflation than other expenses. Accounting for the varying effects of inflation, expenses are broken down into categories based on inflation's impact, as well as other factors.

- Living expenses - non-discretionary, day-to-day expenses subject to inflation, such as groceries, utilities, etc.

- Lifestyle expenses - discretionary expenses subject to inflation, such as travel and entertainment

- Non-standard inflation - expenses (may be discretionary or non-discretionary) that inflate at a different rate than will be used for other expenses. Items such as education and healthcare are shown separately at their corresponding inflation rates.

- Limited life expenses (non-inflationary) - expenses that are fixed in nature with an end date, such as (fixed interest) mortgage payments, car loans, term life insurance payments

- Lifetime expenses - (non-inflationary) - expenses that are fixed in nature with no end date, such as permanent life insurance

Once all the expenses are properly categorized, all the family's data can be entered into the planning software. The first output will be the Year-One Analysis, which will simply be your projected P&L and balance sheet for the year you plan to retire.

It is imperative to once again check the results for errors and see if they make sense. I usually accomplish this by manually calculating the answer on a few individual pieces of data to see if the answers are valid and can pass the *sniff test.* Once again, take nothing for granted.

You now have the current best possible answer as to your income requirements and the value of your assets the year you retire. The numbers will change over time as life deviates from what was forecast. But that's exactly the point. Now that you have a baseline, any changes can easily be incorporated into the analysis and new projections can be obtained.

This process is certainly more involved than using estimates, assumptions, outdated rules of thumb, and black-box calculators. Instead of taking shortcuts to come up with a number that is ultimately useless from a planning perspective, your effort will be rewarded. You are beginning the process of creating your roadmap to the retirement you have worked so hard to achieve.

Step 5: Reviewing Your Current Assets

At the point you enter the transition phase and begin to plan for retirement in earnest, you've probably been in the workforce for perhaps 25, 30, or more years. In that time, you've most likely accumulated an assortment of both retirement and non-retirement assets in multiple accounts. I call this your *bucket of stuff* because, like your basement, it may be filled with things you haven't looked at in a while, can't remember where they came from, and have no idea what they're used for.

Most of the buckets I review contain an assortment of 401(k)s from current and former employers, self-directed traditional and Roth IRAs, brokerage accounts that may contain stock in various companies, some mutual funds, and any number of other investments. You may even own some cash-value life insurance or other insurance products you were sold along the way.

The assets in your bucket need to be used to fund your plan. We must determine if the assets currently in your bucket are appropriate for that purpose or if changes need to be made. In other words, will the current allocation of assets in your bucket allow you to achieve your primary goal of never running out of money? Most likely, they won't.

Concurrent with the planning discussions, I will perform a full review of the family's current holdings. Are the assets appropriate as they move closer to retirement or should some, or all, of the assets be set free to make capital available for reallocation to assets that are appropriate for your purposes?

Let's face it, many people have purchased financial products or investments that were never appropriate for them just because they came across a slick sales presentation. Now is the time to fix past mistakes.

A few common themes emerge when I review the contents of a family's bucket. There are often misconceptions about an asset's function, cost, why they purchased it in the first place, and, most important, who is responsible for managing the account or asset. For instance, **assets in a 401(k) are NOT managed by your current or former employer. They are self-directed, meaning YOU manage them.** This is a common misconception, specifically among those who work or worked for a big-name, blue-chip company, and an often-misunderstood fact could create real problems if you think someone else is looking out for your investments.

Also, rarely do I find that there is any rationale for the management of individual accounts in the bucket. Instead of looking at all of the assets together, there is often no real strategy for tying them together. Many times, I see the only account that has a stated purpose is the *play account* (ugh!)

The tendency is for the bucket to get a lot of attention when the market is doing well and forgotten when the market struggles. Remember, everyone's a genius when the market's going up every day. **You are not a trader!**

While the assets in your bucket may have been appropriate up to this point, they are probably not appropriate to fund your retirement. The assets in your bucket probably focused on growth. Up to this point, during the accumulation phase, that's exactly where they should be. Being too conservative during the accumulation phase, while perhaps comfier during periods of market turmoil, can have disastrous consequences on your long-term plans due to the insidious effects of inflation. Remember, in retirement, you will need your assets to provide more than just growth.

Step 6: Calculating Your Retirement Income Needs

The result of the Year-One Analysis is the total expenses you will incur in your first year of retirement. How will these expenses be funded?

Most people will have some sources of income at retirement. These include Social Security and might include a pension, residual business income, rental income from real estate, etc. These amounts are subtracted from your annual expenses to give the result of the additional income you will need to generate to pay your bills and fund your retirement lifestyle. Your investments and other financial products will be the source of this additional income.

The amount of additional income will need to increase for taxes. This number will not be known until your *Retirement Income Plan* is developed and the tax impact of creating the income is understood. Different investments will be treated differently for tax purposes. Unfortunately, you're about to feel the downside of all those years of deferring tax payments in your IRA and 401(k), as much of your income may be subject to income tax. The tax man wants his cut.

Just as was done in the Year-One Analysis, each subsequent year's projected changes in expenses, as well as the effect of inflation, are included, and the analysis runs out as far as possible. I run this analysis out to age 109, as this is the limit of the software I use. At a minimum, the analysis needs to run through age 100. Your analysis should NEVER stop at life expectancy.

Exhibit 8.3   Additional Income Required Year One of Retirement

Monthly Income	
Social Security	$4,500
Pension	$2,000
Total Income	$6,500
Monthly Expenses	$8,750
Additional Income Required	$2,250

Once completed, the result of this analysis will be the projected income you will need each year of retirement and the basis for the retirement income plan that will provide that income.

Step 7: Planning for Retirement Income Needs

Once you have completed your Year-One and retirement income analyses, you will know the projected amount of income you'll need to generate to support your retirement lifestyle. The next step is to create a retirement income plan to fund those income needs. Your retirement income plan is the strategy that will be employed to allocate your assets in a way that will meet your retirement goals. For most retirees, financial success or failure will be directly attributable to the retirement income plan and strategy that is developed and executed. I will cover the development of your retirement income plan in the next chapter.

Step 8: Breaking your Plan

All the planning to this point has looked only at the scenario where you both live long, healthy lives. While it would be great if this is the outcome, you must plan for other, perhaps more likely, scenarios. What if things don't go quite according to plan?

Each family will have different concerns. What happens if a spouse dies prematurely, there's a health issue, or you need to provide financial support to a parent or child? The possible risks are endless. Just as was done in the Year-One Analysis, I will run different *what-if* scenarios to understand the impact on income or expenses each risk would present. While this sounds like a daunting task, luckily the planning software simplifies the process.

While it's impossible to account for or prepare for all the possible risks that may affect you and your plan, your income plan must be able to function under the most likely scenarios. Managing the risk in your plan will showcase the skill and knowledge of an advisor. In my experience, many will ignore this step. There is very little value in establishing a retirement income plan that will only work if things go perfectly. They seldom do.

The last step in the process is where I attempt to *break* the plan. Throughout the process, it was necessary to use certain assumptions for rates of return, inflation, and asset values. While I limit the risk by using conservative assumptions, market, political, or economic conditions could prove even the most conservative assumptions wrong. Prolonged periods of high inflation or poor market returns can have a disastrous impact on your plan.

Once the retirement income analysis and plan are final, I want to see what conditions would be necessary for the plan to blow up and cease to provide the necessary income. I will accomplish this by running scenarios using increasing rates of inflation and decreasing rates of return until I reach the point where the plan ceases to work. Does the plan explode at rates that have a good chance of occurring? For instance, if the plan works at a rate of inflation of three percent but falls apart at four percent, a highly possible outcome, there's a problem. If, on the other hand, the plan works until a prolonged inflation rate of eight percent, an extremely high rate, there can be a high level of confidence in the plan. The same holds with rates of return.

As you will see in the next chapter, much of this risk can be reduced or eliminated by using the proper solution, investments, and financial products to create your retirement income plan.

Step 9: Execution

Once the Year-One Analysis, retirement income analysis, and the retirement income plan have been completed, tested, stressed, and broken, all that remains is to put your plan in place. At this point, your advisor will execute the transactions necessary to purchase the financial products and put the investment portfolios in place.

Up to this point, everything's just been theory. During execution, your money is going to get allocated to various investments and financial products. Do you know what they are? How they work? Are they liquid? You must make sure you understand your income plan and the products being used to execute it. Don't be afraid to ask questions. A misunderstanding at this point could be costly.

This chapter offered a very basic walk through of the financial planning for retirement process. Once again, I must point out that while the steps may be the same, your plan will be unique. There are no generic plans, financial products, or investment strategies that will work in every case.

While you may be tempted to take shortcuts, please don't. The process is too important. A (very) little effort now, ten or fifteen years before retirement, could be the difference between living the retirement of your dreams and a financial nightmare.

CHAPTER 9

The Retirement Income Conundrum

The best methodology for producing retirement income, like so many other topics in this business, is a subject of tremendous disagreement among advisors. The stock guys favor the use of a portfolio of market products to create your income solution, while the insurance guys favor the use of insurance products, specifically annuities and cash value life insurance.

While the methodology selected and advocated by any advisor may very well be determined by the firm they work for and the products they are licensed to sell, there are nevertheless valid arguments on both sides. Putting aside the sales motivation of the advisor for a moment, the debate over retirement income is one that requires an unbiased analysis. If you're going to execute a retirement income plan, you'll ultimately need to purchase - or be sold - a solution. I guess it's time to settle another argument.

Measuring a Retirement Income Plan

Deciding on the retirement income solution you will use is probably one of the most important financial decisions you will ever make. Up to this point, bad financial decisions could be fixed. While you're working, there is always time and a source of income. Once you stop working, a bad financial decision can be disastrous.

When the market misbehaves, the effects are felt immediately. The effects of a bad retirement income plan, however, are insidious. The plan may be in trouble, and you might never feel a thing - until it's too late. Events that occur years before you sense any problem can doom your plan— and you'll never see it coming. You get one chance at this. You need to make sure you get it right. But, what's right? Which methodology will give you the best chance to achieve your retirement goals?

There are articles written, almost daily, that attempt to settle the retirement income debate. These articles are usually written by advisors, financial pundits, or financial firms that have strong feelings, and usually a strong profit motive, to prove the methodology they advocate is superior. Most of the debate on the topic attempts to use mathematics and historical return data to prove that, based on the past, one method will produce more income while you're alive and a higher legacy to pass on to your heirs, after your death.

These analyses usually look at the market and economy using average returns, average interest rates, and average rates of inflation, over long periods of time. Not only are these analyses mathematically misleading, but they also - perhaps intentionally - attempt to lessen, deflect, or eliminate the memory of events like Black Monday, the dot-com bust, and the financial crisis of 2008.

Historical analysis is only one measure of the viability of an income methodology. I would argue that it's not a very good one. Remember, past performance is no indication of future results. The choice of an income solution is not a decision that should be based on the repeatability of a theory of historical averages; this is strictly an issue of risk management.

The success of a retirement income strategy will be determined by how well it's able to manage the risks you'll face in retirement, under all market conditions. If you remember from chapter 6, the risks you'll encounter are substantially more than just market risk. How do the various methods of generating retirement income manage longevity risk, inflation, and sequence of returns risk? Who will be responsible for managing the risk? Once again, first we manage risk.

In addition to its ability to manage risk, a retirement income plan must be judged not only on the math, but also on how easy it will be to live with, both logistically and emotionally. A plan that works in averages will be of little use when the market or economic SPAM hits the fan. Theory is great, but will you be able to withstand the psychological impact of another market or economic upheaval when you're no longer working? *Math may be unemotional, but people aren't.*

Once again, you're not an investment manager or a cash manager. For most people, their primary concern is getting their retirement paycheck every month, regardless of market or economic conditions, without having to perform elaborate financial gymnastics.

Will a portfolio of stocks, bonds, and other market instruments be the ultimate solution for your retirement income plan, or will insurance products prove superior? Or, perhaps the answer lies elsewhere.

Before we can decide if either method, by itself, can satisfy your retirement income needs, I will analyze both. This analysis will be based not on hypothetical, historical performance, but on risk and one's ability to live with the solution.

The Investment Solution

While the products used may differ among advisors, the investment solution usually entails a strategy of taking periodic or systematic withdrawals from a portfolio to fund your income needs.

While systematic withdrawals are nothing new, the solution was popularized by Richard Bengen in his 1994 article, *Determining Withdrawal Rates using Historical Data.*[19] In the article, Bengen analyzed various annual withdrawal rates from a variety of portfolios of stocks and bonds to see which combination would yield the highest probability of not running out of money. He used historical market returns of stocks and bonds for his analysis. The result of Bengen's work is what has become known as the 4 Percent Rule.

Used by many advisors as the basis for their retirement income solution, the 4 Percent Rule generates income by withdrawing four percent from your portfolio during the first year of retirement. According to Bengen, the portfolio should consist of 50 percent stocks and 50 percent intermediate-term bonds. The portfolio should be rebalanced each year.

Withdrawals in subsequent years are increased by the rate of inflation from the previous year. For example, if inflation this year (the first year of retirement) was three percent, next year's withdrawal rate would be 4.12 percent.

According to Bengen, there was no case that this method would not have led to a portfolio life of less than 33 years, and in most cases, the portfolios lasted 50 years or longer[20].

Proponents of this methodology point to the results of Bengen's work as proof that keeping all your money allocated in the market will prevent you from going broke. This is indeed a significant selling point. Given the probability of growth in the portfolio, a higher income value and a higher legacy value may be available. Also, investment balances are liquid and accessible by the investor at any time. As you will see, this is not necessarily the case in the insurance solution.

If we take all this at face value, the investment solution, adequately executed, seems like it may work. Not so fast! There's a boatload of issues that need to be understood.

Many in the financial advice industry still take Bengen's work as a financial law or at least a very well used rule-of-thumb. I find it amazing that for an issue of such importance, I have NEVER (seriously never, not once) met a person in the industry who has read the article. Most assume that four percent is some universal mathematical law on par with $E=mc^2$.

Bengen himself points out many of the issues in the appendix of the article that, in my opinion, limit the accuracy in a real-world scenario[21]. As this is not meant to be a review or critique of the article, I will simply say; *past performance is no guarantee of future results.* The reliance on historical data is a significant issue as returns, especially in the bond market, are much different today than they were when the article was written. Tomorrow's market will be much different from those in the past. The events of the financial crisis of 2008 were thought to be impossible, until they happened.

While Bengen's work was interesting and made some noteworthy points, if one merely reads the article, they will see that it was never the author's intention, in my opinion, that this become law. The absence of any scientific method has once again failed the financial industry.

Some current studies of systematic withdrawal rates put the safe withdrawal rate, the rate that would prevent you from going broke, closer to two percent, based on recent interest rates. But, let's assume for a moment that the 4 percent rule is mathematically valid. How does the investment solution of systematic withdrawals stand up when we look at risk and liveability from a logistical and psychological standpoint?

As I discussed in chapter 6, risk is a fact of life that must be understood and managed. Eliminating all risk from any income solution is impossible. For the risk which remains, can it be mitigated, and who is responsible for its management? Surprises are a terrible thing when you have no ability to recover.

The investment solution assumes income will be taken from a portfolio of stocks and bonds on a periodic basis. Because you never know what the market will do in the future, sequence of returns risk will be a present danger for at least the first five years of your retirement. If you recall from exhibit 6.1, the year you decide to retire will make a big difference. There is, however, no way to know in advance if you made a good or bad decision. A down, or even flat, market at the beginning of retirement may doom your plan later on, with no good way to recover.

There are no guarantees with a portfolio of market assets. As we are living longer lives, the possibility of outliving our assets becomes a harsh reality. The investment solution gives no protection for longevity risk, especially if you live longer than perhaps your plan anticipated. Once your assets are gone, they're gone.

Under an investment solution, the responsibility for managing the dual risks of longevity and sequence of returns falls on you. Even if you're using an advisor to manage your assets, you are still the one taking and ultimately managing the risk. Even the best, most well-meaning advisor has no control over market returns and how long you live. While you may be willing to accept and manage the risk at age 65, will you still be able to at 80, when perhaps your cognitive abilities are starting to slow?

Inflation is one area where the investment solution shines. Most portfolio assets are designed for growth. If we assume no material changes to cash flow over the years, the growth in the portfolio should be able to more than compensate for inflation.

The liveability of the investment solution may be where the real problems lie. Mathematics, historical returns, and financial theory are fine in a textbook, but what happens when you put theory into practice and things don't go according to plan?

To illustrate this point, let's assume you retired in January 2008. The markets have recovered from the dot-com bust, your house is worth many times what you thought possible, and life looks good. Then the unthinkable happens. The market plummets, and the value of your house sinks back to more realistic levels. Now what?

Many proponents of the investment solution, including Bengen, admit that, to ensure the longevity of your assets, adjustments to spending may have to occur after bad markets.

Bengen called these *black hole* events.[22] In fact, many investment solutions I have reviewed are based on adjusting spending the year following a down markct. Will you be able to cut your spending each time the market is down? Would you want to? Market disruptions happen all the time and can happen at any time.

The psychological factors are perhaps the most important. When things get stressful, logic tends to go out the window. Thankfully, most families I have met didn't panic out of the market in 2008. Some did. How different would your reaction be if, when retired, other than Social Security, your investments were your only source of income? Could you stay the course?

Another area where psychological factors come into play is with liquidity. Some advisors point to the liquidity of the assets under an investment solution as a significant benefit. If you need cash, you can get some in short order. This benefit, however, comes at a price. Many retirees either focus on enjoying today and overspend, running the risk of running out of money later, or they are so worried about running out of money that they never spend a dime on anything that isn't essential. Neither is a good result.

Investments, as a stand-alone solution for retirement income, have many shortcomings that the average retiree may not be aware. Unfortunately, as I've stated on a few other occasions, Wall Street is where the bulk of our information and understanding comes from in our market-centric world, and thus many assume this is the only solution. In my opinion, relying solely on an investment solution for retirement income is far too risky.

The Insurance Solution

The retirement income solution advocated by the insurance guys usually entails converting all or a significant portion of your assets into insurance products.

Most often, this would be the purchase of some form of annuity and possibly cash value life insurance.

There are multiple types of annuities available. I will cover annuities in some detail in chapter 11. For the sake of this analysis, let's look at the general form of an annuity. The simplest way to think of an annuity is as a pension. In exchange for a sum of money, the insurance company will give you a stream of income that is guaranteed to last for a specified period, for your lifetime, or for the life of both you and a spouse. Purchasing an annuity is essentially creating your own personal pension.

Cash value life insurance has uses that go beyond the death benefit. The cash value of the policy can be borrowed against tax-free to use as one piece of retirement income. I will go deeper into the various uses for life insurance in chapter 13.

From my experience, it seems the choice of an insurance solution is directly related to the firm employing the insurance guy. This should come as no surprise. The compensation of captive agents, those who work for an insurance company, is usually heavily dependent on the amount of cash value (typically whole life) insurance they sell. The solution they present will usually be weighted heavily toward a life insurance product. Independent agents, who have no production requirements, are more inclined to use annuities in their solutions. Remember, the insurance guys and the stock guys who operate as brokers operate under the suitability standard. They are not required to act in your best interest at this point!

The insurance solution would seem to be appealing. In the case of annuities, in exchange for an amount of cash, you will receive income guaranteed for life. This income cannot go down, may go up, and, except for variable annuities, is not subject to market risk. The life insurance cash value can then be used as a supplemental source of income, if needed, and to provide a legacy. That sounds pretty good.

By using actuarial science and the law of large numbers, the insurance companies can pool their risk and spread it across their entire universe of policyholders. This allows them to offer benefits and guarantees not available with other asset classes. With the benefit of guaranteed, lifetime income, you can significantly reduce the risk of longevity by shifting it back to the insurance company.

Sequence of returns risk is also significantly reduced under the insurance solution as the contractual lifetime income guarantees are not dependent on market returns. Positive market returns can enhance the income of certain annuities and the cash value of certain types of life insurance, but regardless of market direction, the contractual guarantees will always be available. Once again, I'll get deeper into the products later.

The major risk with the insurance solution is from inflation. Contrary to the sales pitches of many of the insurance sales guys, insurance products are NOT designed to provide stock-market-like growth. Dumping a significant portion of your nest egg into an annuity will most likely produce a very attractive amount of income. However, ten years into retirement, that income may not seem as attractive when the effects of inflation start eating away at its purchasing power.

The insurance solution's greatest asset, in my opinion, is one that is hard to measure from an analysis standpoint. The guaranteed lifetime income removes many of the psychological and logistical barriers of the investment solution. When you enter retirement, you will know how much income you will be receiving each month. This number may go up over time, but in most cases, cannot go down. Income guarantees act as a permission slip allowing retirees, who are concerned about their money to the point of not spending, to go ahead and spend as their plan allows. It will also keep the spenders in check, as they will know their income in advance and not run the risk of having to decrease spending should a year or so of negative market returns occur.

On the negative side, money put into an annuity is not liquid. Depending on the type of annuity you purchase, there may be some liquidity available, but taking any money out of these products in a manner other than dictated by the contract will lead to a reduction in the contractual guarantee amounts. So, while the insurance guy may tell you there's liquidity, it comes at a hefty price.

In my opinion, the most significant drawback to the insurance solution comes from the questionable sales tactics of many of the advisors that sell insurance products. Many insurance producers play on your fear of the stock market to entice the sale of insurance products. They misrepresent the growth potential of the products by using sales illustrations that paint an overly rosy picture of the anticipated future value or amount of income that will be available. Their sales presentations are scripted, polished, and well-rehearsed to play on your fears and overcome your objections.

As I pointed out earlier, insurance guys who are not securities licensed are forbidden from recommending that you sell securities to fund their solution. It still amazes me that they are allowed to roll over a 401(k), IRA, or brokerage account into insurance products, supposedly without making a recommendation to sell those investments.

Most people I come across have at least some understanding of the stock market. Very few understand anything about insurance products. Insurance products are extremely complex financial instruments that must be thoroughly understood before purchase. Unfortunately, many of the sales guys I have met, lack the financial knowledge to understand them themselves.

To be fair, not all who are just insurance licensed are bad. In fact, there are many reputable and knowledgeable insurance producers. I have had the pleasure to meet and work with many of them. They are usually very easy to spot. They will thoroughly explain their products and their proper use without resorting to sales tactics and uncomfortable closing techniques. They understand that insurance products should be purchased, not sold.

And the Winner is...

The preceding analysis looked at a general case of both the investment and insurance solution. I do not doubt that most advisors will attempt to debunk my analysis by pointing to some magic financial product that they alone have access to that does everything and manages every risk. Such a product doesn't exist. If it did, you'd probably know, as something as miraculous as the perfect financial product would be well reported. While the products that individual advisors use may change, the risks inherent in either solution are hard to eliminate without looking elsewhere.

Neither solution is perfect; they both have their pros and cons. The investment solution has the potential to provide tremendous upside if the market cooperates, but, with no guarantees, you also have the possibility of going broke. While inflation shouldn't be an issue, the responsibility for managing longevity and sequence of returns falls squarely on your shoulders. Is it realistic to assume you want, or are qualified, to manage that risk? Will this uncertainty cause you to be too conservative with your spending, or will your big number cause you to overspend? Also, could you handle the psychological stress of a rollercoaster market when you're no longer working and have no chance to recover?

The insurance solution may seem to offer more protection. Having the opportunity for guaranteed lifetime income with no exposure to the market transfers the responsibility for managing longevity and sequence of returns risk to the insurance company. Inflation risk is still yours to manage, and that will be a significant concern if you take full advantage of the longevity protection and live a very long life.

Since market risk shouldn't be an issue with insurance solutions, there is no worry that you'll need to adjust your spending after a year or so of down markets. The stock market is no longer a stressor. You'll always know the amount of your retirement paycheck. Income surprises should not be an issue. However, the absence of liquidity could present a real problem should emergencies or other cash needs arise. The most significant drawbacks of the insurance solution may be the complexity of the products and the questionable sales tactics of many of the people who sell them. The perfect income plan could be a disaster if your solution contains sub-standard products you don't understand.

It's at this point during a presentation, with the preceding exhibit written on the board, that I'll ask the question: *Which income solution would you rather have for your retirement plan?* I intentionally ask the question in a manner that makes the audience assume they need to make a choice, a very common tactic for the sales guys.

Exhibit 9.1   Risk Management of Income Solutions Summary

Insurance Solution	Risk	Investment Solution
✗	**Inflation**	✓
✓	**Longevity**	✗
✓	**Sequence of Returns**	✗

The discussion that follows almost always focuses on the risk management provided by the insurance solution. Gaining the peace of mind the guarantees of the insurance solution offer seems to be much more important than losing the growth potential of the investment solution. Amazingly, in my experience, even the most hardcore fans of the stock market begrudgingly admit that the insurance solution would be their choice. So, the winner is... neither! It was a trick question.

You MUST stop thinking that investing is an either/ or decision. It's not, but that's the path most sales guys will lead you down. No law states that you can't have a retirement income solution that contains both investment and insurance products. Diversification, the most misused and misunderstood word in the financial lexicon, applies to much more than just the percentage of stocks and bonds you have in your portfolio.

So, what's the answer?

CHAPTER 10

A Long Life Funded

Running out of money in retirement is a scary prospect. In fact, in many recent surveys, it's the number one retirement concern of adults of every age group. In one survey, those asked fear running out of money in retirement more than they fear death[23]! That's an outcome that just can't be allowed to happen.

One of the problems with using an income solution that focuses on a single asset class is that most assets are horrible multitaskers. Investment solutions containing only portfolios of stocks rely, for the most part, on assets that are growth-oriented, leaving you at risk for longevity and sequence of returns issues. Insurance solutions focus on providing a stream of income, creating a potential long-term problem with inflation. Either solution, by itself, leaves a tremendous amount of risk that, if left unmanaged, could lead to disaster.

A fundamental flaw in the logic of many advisors stems from the two-phase retirement model discussed in chapter 7. The model assumes that in the accumulation phase, the objective is the growth of your assets—the big number—and on the day you retire, you jump into the distribution phase where income—the small number—is the objective. The problem with this thinking is that, in retirement, you need your assets to provide more than just income.

A Model for Your Retirement Income Solution

Retirement income solution may be a bit of a misnomer. While our ultimate goal is to produce an income that you can't out-live, the model will need to provide for the other functions your money will need to serve in retirement. In retirement, your dollars will need to do more than just provide income. In addition to income, a portion of your assets will be needed to provide for growth, liquidity, and protection.

A coach will give his team the best chance of winning by using his players in the positions for which they are best suited. Why should your retirement income solution be any different? Wouldn't it make sense to align the various financial needs you'll have in retirement (or any point in your life, for that matter) with the financial products that are best suited to fill those needs? *The retirement income model* requires the use of the assets that are best suited for each task. What a novel concept!

The purpose of the model is to provide a consistent frame-work for developing your retirement income solution. Unlike the sales systems of the product jockeys which are designed to walk you down a path to their desired result of the sale of a specific product, the model has no preconceived result

Exhibit 10.1   The Four Financial Needs

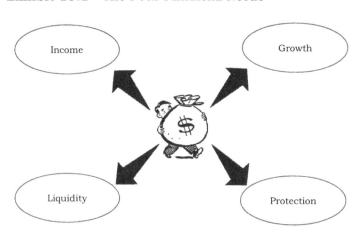

in mind. The model is a set of principles, strategies, and a framework for developing your retirement income solution that ensures you have the optimal strategy, based on your situation, to reach your retirement goals.

It's important to remember that there are no generic answers. Unlike answers from the free-advice crowd, your solution will be based on your goals, current financial situation, time to retirement, and many other items and issues. Your solution will be unique to you.

Income

The first financial need I address is your income. After all, without income, you have no retirement. Your income is your retirement paycheck. Remember, one of the goals is to enter retirement as stress free as possible. You don't want to have to figure out where you're getting the money to pay your bills. You've been living off a paycheck your entire adult life; retirement should be no different.

If you recall from chapter 8, your income needs entering retirement are calculated during the planning process. They are calculated by taking your estimated expenses and subtracting all your known sources of income. These will include Social Security, any pensions you may be fortunate to have, business or real estate income, etc. The result is your *income gap* or the amount of income you'll need to produce with your retirement income solution (refer back to exhibit 8.4.)

Next, I refer back to your plan and analyze the expenses for the first five or so years of your retirement. Are the expenses projected to be fairly level during that time, or will they be increasing for more than just inflation? The goal is not to match the income solution exactly with your expenses, but to provide an income with a bit of cushion. Expenses fluctuate from month to month. You'll want to produce more income than is needed to cover the fluctuations. Excess income generated in the first few years can be used to cover shortfalls later on. The result of this analysis is *your base income* need and the starting point of your income solution.

Now you have to decide how you'll deploy your assets to create this income stream. Which income solution - investments or insurance - is better suited to produce this income? Hint: Wouldn't it be nice to have a pension to provide this income?

When you create this income, it must satisfy at least the following requirements:

- Periodic (usually monthly) payments; a paycheck
- Payments MUST be guaranteed to continue for as long as one spouse is living.
- Payment amount MUST be fixed or possibly increase, but it can NEVER decrease due to adverse market conditions.

If you've been paying attention, you'll recognize that the insurance solution is the answer for your income needs. Insurance products, primarily annuities, are designed to provide the guaranteed, lifetime income that you require. Using the proper annuity essentially allows you to create your very own personal pension.

Providing guaranteed streams of income are what annuities are designed to do.

Yeah, I know what you've heard about annuities. Haven't I already shown that most of what you've heard on any financial topic is nothing more than self-serving sales speak from the product pushers that want you to buy their product instead? Well, in this case, some of what you've heard may be true! I'll cover annuities in the next chapter.

If one of your goals is to never run out of money in retirement, an annuity may be your best defense. The guaranteed lifetime income will significantly reduce or eliminate longevity risk; as long as you're breathing, you keep getting paid. Also, since the payments can never decrease or be negatively impacted by the stock market, sequence of returns risk should not be an issue. For this income, you've significantly reduced the dual risks of longevity and sequence of returns, leaving only inflation to manage.

As you progress through retirement, your income needs will change. These changes have been anticipated in the planning process. As your income requirements increase, one strategy is to purchase additional annuities to provide the additional income you need, in effect giving yourself a raise in your paycheck. Your situation may provide many other ways to produce the additional income. Once again, the model is a framework that may provide many possible solutions, not a selling system, which only has one.

Depending on the income need, the cash value from life insurance may be available for use. You can borrow the cash value in a permanent life insurance policy, tax free, to provide another source of retirement income. While certainly not appropriate for everyone, permanent life insurance can provide much more than a death benefit. Properly structured, it can provide tax-free income, protection for long-term care needs, and a legacy for your heirs. Life insurance can be a key player in your retirement portfolio. I will discuss life insurance in more detail in chapter 13.

Another tool for producing retirement income is the use of bonds. I must urge caution here. Contrary to what most of us have been led to believe our entire adult lives, bonds are not simple instruments without risk. In fact, in certain cases, they can carry greater risk to your retirement than stocks. While a full analysis of the bond market is beyond the scope of this book, there are a few key points of which you must be aware.

First, bonds are extremely complicated. There are many types, including government, municipal, corporate, agency, zero coupon, etc. Each type of bond will have different attributes, uses, and tax treatment, which can vary based on where you live.

The creation, analysis, and management of bond portfolios is an extremely specialized field. For many bond managers, the creation of a suitably diversified portfolio requires a minimum investment of $500,000, an amount which may be out of reach for many while still having enough assets remaining for the other needs we will discuss. Regardless of what you may be told, bond portfolios and strategies are not something that Joe Broker Guy can handle.

Second, bonds will be subject to interest-rate risk upon maturity. While a portfolio of bonds can be created to generate your desired amount of income, each time a bond matures, it must be reinvested at the prevailing interest rates. In an environment of falling interest rates, this could mean a reduction in your monthly income, possibly creating an income shortfall. Will your remaining assets be able to pick up the slack?

Third, bond mutual funds are NOT the same as a portfolio of bonds and are NOT a replacement for a properly managed and diversified portfolio of bonds. I will get more into mutual funds in chapter 12.

Funding your income needs is certainly the most complex part of the process. Most solutions will require you to understand complex financial products and make difficult decisions. Once again, it is imperative that you understand what's going on. This is no place for the bobblehead.

Through this process, we've created the base income you'll need as you begin retirement and addressed two of the three major retirement risks. Creating a regular paycheck using annuities will also reduce the psychological and logistical stress of entering retirement as your retirement paycheck will arrive every month, guaranteed.

Growth

Over the course of retirement, your income needs will change. Your income streams will begin to feel the effects of inflation. At some point, you'll need additional income as changes to your cash needs from either planned or unexpected expenses arise. Your retirement goals may also change, and you may require funds to make them a reality.

Income assets are generally not built to provide growth. While Social Security, still contains a cost of living adjustment (COLA), I have not reviewed a private pension in a long time that still contains a COLA. Also, the income generated from the annuities that are used to fund your base income needs will, in most cases, be fixed.

While your income assets are paying the bills, other assets need to continue to grow so they'll be available for the future. When needed, these assets can be used to fund planned or unplanned individual purchases or financial needs or, as discussed in the last section, be converted to annuities to produce additional income. Since you've done your planning, much of these cash flows have already been anticipated.

In short, you will use your growth assets for inflation protection and additional cash needs - both planned and unplanned. Since your growth assets don't need to be continually called upon to provide income, they can remain invested without the stress of market volatility.

With the aid of your plan and, as you will see, the proper use of liquidity, you will determine the timing of withdrawals from your investments, meaning, in most cases, you shouldn't need to tap your investments when the market is down. You should never need to take money from your growth assets *today*. Having the ability to control the timing of withdrawals from your investment accounts further reduces sequence of returns risk. That's one risk that shouldn't be a problem!

The growth of assets properly invested in the market should, over time, far outpace the effects of inflation on your income. As an indication, since 1950, the S&P 500 has returned 7 percent, accounting for dividends and net of inflation. Look at that—another risk has been managed and taken off the table!

How you invest your growth assets is vitally important. You may be pitched an array of tactics, products, mutual funds, etc., from your advisor. Once again, it's not about product or tactics; it's about strategy. Most investors are unknowingly relegated to the world of retail investing - even if you use an advisor. I will go over the proper investment methodology in chapter 12. For now, simply ask yourself this: Regardless of the size of your nest-egg, would you rather invest like the masses or invest like the wealthy? The choice will be yours.

While keeping a large portion of your assets invested in the market may worry some of you that are petrified of market risk, I will show you shortly how the proper use of liquidity will drastically reduce this concern. After all, the market is where the growth is.

Liquidity

As part of your retirement income solution, a certain amount of assets will need to remain liquid to pay for those unexpected expenses that come up periodically. Some refer to it as your emergency fund. Our parents and grandparents called it the rainy-day fund.

The proper assets to use for your liquidity allocation have become the subject of some debate. Some advisors consider funds invested in brokerage accounts to be appropriate to include in a client's liquidity allocation since they can be sold and available in as little as a day or so, depending on the asset. This is a very convenient determination for the advisor, and utterly wrong. Assets earmarked for your liquidity allocation should not be subject to market fluctuations. You need to know that when you need the money, it will be there. You cannot risk needing to tap your funds only to find out that their value has decreased due to a down market.

Many formulas or rules of thumb can be used to estimate the amount of money you need to keep liquid at any time. In retirement, the number is less about crunching a formula and more about what amount will make you feel secure. As is always the case, each of us is different and so is the answer.

For example, I work with two families that have very different liquidity needs. One lives in a 175-year- old historic home, and the other lives in a brand-new retirement community where he pays one monthly fee that takes care of all maintenance issues. He doesn't even need to change light bulbs. Which of these families do you think needs more liquidity? For each of these families, a discussion took place to find the optimal amount of liquidity for their situation.

There are uses for your liquidity account other than just as an emergency fund. As I will show in a moment, it will be used as a funding method for inflation and a way to lessen the effects of market risk on your portfolio of growth assets.

Using Liquidity to Manage Inflation

I've already explained how the assets that are invested for growth will be used to give protection from inflation. However, taking funds directly from your growth assets is inefficient unless you are taking systematic withdrawals, and we've seen the issues that those can create. Needing to sell investments during periods of extreme market volatility can add undue stress, even if the amounts are small. You should always strive to buy on sale, not sell. When the market is down, assets are on sale. That's not the time to sell.

To eliminate this issue and make funding for inflation easier, I use a method that sets up a *reserve* for inflation in your liquidity account. If your expenses increase due to inflation, funds are readily available. The following is a simplification of the process, but I'm sure you'll get the picture.

Let's assume that your annual expenses are $60,000 and inflation is projected to be 3 percent. That means the cost of inflation for two years is $3,654. Let's round that up to $5,000. If you add $5,000 to your liquidity account, you'll have the funds available to cover over two and a half years' worth of inflation without touching your growth assets.

Why is this important? Because you never need to touch your growth assets *today*. In the absence of any other financial need, you can decide when to take money from your investments to refund the liquidity account. You won't have to sell if your investments are on sale. Selling small amounts to cover the periodic needs of inflation can be expensive as commissions and fees can start to add up. Also, your investments will most likely produce some dividends and interest that will be available to increase monthly income without adding additional cost.

When you eliminate the need to constantly access your investment accounts, your focus will shift to other, more enjoyable thoughts, like your retirement. See, market risk, while unavoidable, doesn't need to be scary.

Protection

Stuff happens! Most of the time, it will happen at the worst times. The possibility that some unforeseen event can derail your retirement plans must be addressed.

One bad day can never be allowed to turn into a lifetime of financial hardship. If you recall from chapter 6, *event risk* can

Exhibit 10.2   Funding Inflation

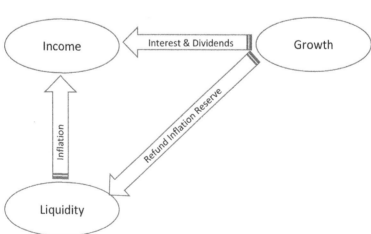

strike at any time. The goal of your protection is to deploy a portion of your retirement assets with the purpose of protecting the remainder of your assets.

Each family will have issues and concerns that will require some form of protection. Please review exhibit 6.3. How many of these risks might affect you? Once again, your family's situation is different from others. Your issues and concerns need to be thoroughly understood, analyzed, and adequately addressed. Are there other risks that can affect your retirement that were not listed?

Having a financial plan that works in only the best situation is of little value when some unforeseen event occurs. Your financial plan should have been stress tested for the premature death of a spouse or the need for long-term care to understand the effect either would have on your plans.

Many people underestimate the financial impact of the premature death of a spouse. They wrongly assume that, from a financial perspective only, the reduction of costs associated with the deceased will make up for any lost benefits. This may not be the case.

As we are living longer, the need for long-term care is increasing and getting more expensive. Current estimates place the likelihood of needing long-term care at 44 percent for men and 58 percent for women[24]. Other estimates state that 70 percent of people over the age of 70 will eventually require some form of long-term care[25]. The 2017 median cost (national) of a private room in a nursing home was $97,455, an increase of 5.5 percent from the previous year and a 50 percent increase from 2004[26]. How much might this cost if you require long-term care in 20 or 30 years? How will you cover this cost without going broke in the process?

Many Americans wrongly believe that the government will cover most of the cost of long-term care. Unless you qualify for Medicaid, they won't! A strategy to provide for long-term care needs should be discussed to prevent the depletion of your assets should a long-term care need arise.

While Insurance Guy would be happy to sell you policies to cover all your risks, this is an impractical methodology that will almost certainly make you insurance rich and cash poor. Some event risks can be self-insured, meaning that you will be able to cover their expense from your assets. Others will require the purchase of insurance to mitigate properly. The introduction of hybrid insurance products makes it possible to manage both the risk of premature death and the need for long-term care in the same policy. I will discuss these further in chapter 13.

Through the proper execution of your income solution, you have managed the major risks of inflation, longevity, and sequence of returns. By properly allocating for protection, you will reduce the possibility that an unforeseen event can derail your plans.

Putting Your Plan into Action

Like so many other topics I've covered, the argument over the best retirement income solution is nothing more than a bunch of sales guys attempting to mark their territory. As I have shown, they're both wrong - and right. Choosing the optimal income solution to fund your retirement needs is far more complicated than just purchasing a product or portfolio. For a solution to work, it will require the coordination of the proper assets and strategies, along with a properly constructed financial plan.

Equally important is your ability to live with the plan. You must remember that you do not want to worry each month about how you will fund next month's bills, where the money will come from in an emergency, or what happens if the market craters. In fact, I'm sure there are many things you can find yourself worrying about in a poorly conceived income plan. Too often, advisors spend so much time trying to educate prospects about the products they are selling that they forget about the most important thing. How will you live with this plan?

As I've said a few times before, this is an exercise in personal finance, not a course in higher level Calculus. Even with the inclusion of some complex financial products, you should still understand how your income plan works under all market and economic conditions.

At this point, you should be having that ah-ha moment. You should see how everything I've discussed so far is coming together. The work that you did in the planning process and your new understanding of risk management should give you much better control and comfort with your retirement prospects. It's certainly better than a ballpark estimate, the results of a random online calculator, or the consequence of some selling system.

Now that your planning is complete, it's time to execute. All the work you've done to this point will result in nothing more than a useless stack of paper unless your plan is properly executed. For this, you'll need to put your dollars to work.

As I've discussed many times in this book, there's far too much misinformation, bad information, and outdated information being used to justify product sales. It's vitally important that your choice of financial products and strategy be guided by knowledge and not advertising or the self-interest of advisors or product jockeys. Up to this point, mistakes could be fixed by simply revising an analysis and rerunning a report. Once your investments are placed and financial products purchased, mistakes can be expensive and potentially hard to correct.

In the chapters that follow, I will discuss the proper products, investments, and concepts required to execute your financial plan properly. Much of what I will discuss will contradict conventional wisdom and be the opposite of *what you've heard*. But please remember, the model can lead to many different solutions. My goal, as always, is to give you the information to cut through the noise of the product pushers and free-advice crowd to make informed, educated decisions.

Part III

Execution

CHAPTER 11

Annuities: Complex but Worth the Effort

Of all the heated debates in the world of finance, none is hotter than the debate over annuities. I can't think of another financial product that elicits such strong emotions on both sides of the argument. Many consumers have similarly strong feelings. "I've heard annuities are..." is a very common response when I bring up the subject. When pressed, most people are simply unsure of what an annuity is, how they work, or how one can fit into their financial plan.

Annuities represent some of the best, and worst, the financial world has to offer. The proper annuity used in the right situation can add value and certainty to a financial plan in a manner that's hard to achieve with other financial products. Conversely, improperly used, annuities can be expensive financial products that do little more than putting a big commission into the pocket of the sales guy. Probably the biggest issue with annuities is that they are complex financial products that, in many cases, neither the haters nor the annuity sellers truly understand.

It is important that you understand the various types of annuities, how they work, and how they fit into your retirement income solution. First, I need to discuss the reasons, both valid and invalid, why annuities are a topic of such heated debate. Then, I can show how they can be an invaluable piece of your income solution.

Why All the Hate?

Without spending too much time on the subject, there are three main reasons why such strong feelings surround the sale and use of annuities. There are also a few other factors that will be discussed when I review the individual types of annuities.

First, as is always the case, advisors and financial firms that don't sell annuities do everything in their power to convince the public that they're evil. The truth here is annuities are a competing product that takes sales away from whatever it is they're selling. Their efforts usually involve sales collateral that attempts to *educate* the public about the problems with annuities. As I've previously discussed the education issue, you should be able to spot and dismiss this tactic.

Second, most of the heavy hating comes from those that are discussing variable annuities (VAs). Part of the problem with annuities is that there are many different types. Each type of annuity has its own characteristics and uses. Unfortunately, when annuities are discussed, they are referred to simply as annuities and not by the individual type. Thus, all annuities get lumped together. As you will see, there are vast differences between VAs and other annuities. Some of the hate is certainly warranted here. I will get deeper into VAs later in this chapter.

The third, and perhaps the biggest, reason for the negativity surrounding annuities is the questionable sales tactics of the annuity product pushers. Let's face it, if all you sell are annuities, then everyone you meet must need an annuity. Some of these guys continually misrepresent their products and misinform and confuse their prospects. Once they get the bobblehead going, they have a sale.

Annuities are complex products. Many people who have previously purchased annuities have no idea what they bought. I regularly review previous annuity purchases with families I am beginning to advise and have NEVER seen an instance where they completely understood what they purchased. In most cases, their understanding of the product is not even close to reality. Whether this is the result of a lack of education or understanding during the sales process, unethical sales tactics, or all of the above is hard to tell. However, I would assume that if it wasn't an ethical issue, I eventually would come across a family that understood what they purchased. I'm still waiting for that to happen!

I could go on about this topic, but I'm sure you get the point. Many of these issues can be avoided if you, as the purchaser, had a better understanding of these products, the major types, how they work, and how they should, and shouldn't, be used. Let's get you that knowledge.

The Immediate Annuity

An immediate annuity, also commonly referred to as a Single Premium Immediate Annuity or SPIA, is used to transform a lump sum of money into a guaranteed income stream. In simple terms, it's like buying a monthly pension check. You give a lump sum to the insurance company, and they start paying you - usually within 30 days.

The amount of income you will get for a given amount of premium dollars depends primarily on four factors: interest rates, your age, your sex, and the desired payout period. The insurance company will use actuarial calculations to figure your payments.

They immediate annuities are often used for a lifetime income, they can also be purchased for a joint- life, that is the lives of both you and your spouse. They can also be purchased for a specific period, referred to as a period-certain, of five, ten, fifteen years, etc. In these cases, payments will cease at the end of the defined period. If you die before the end of the defined period, payments will continue to your heirs. Combinations of life with period-certain payments are also available. These period-certain annuities are useful for different purposes, including funding the first years of retirement until other sources of income such as Social Security begin.

The advantages of immediate annuities are that, in addition to being relatively simple, they pay an immediate, fixed, guaranteed payment for your lifetime or another chosen period.

What's the downside? Improperly used, there's a few. The process of *annuitization* converts an annuity investment into a stream of periodic payments. Once annuitization occurs - immediately in an immediate annuity - the process cannot be reversed. You, in effect, give up control of your money to receive the income stream. Annuitization could be a problem if you need a lump sum of cash in the future and is the main reason you never put all your money in an annuity of any type.

Also, if you elect life or joint-life payments, without a period certain, once you or you and your spouse die, payments stop. Similar to most pensions, in the case of a tragedy early in retirement, the money invested would go back to the insurance company and not your heirs.

The final issue to be aware of is that since you receive fixed payments, the longer you're receiving payments, the greater the effect inflation will have on purchasing power. What seemed like a large payment when it started will seem much smaller after ten or twenty years. This fact should have been accounted for in your plan and income solution.

In today's market, insurance companies have developed immediate annuities that solve many of these issues. While these new products may sound appealing, the inclusion of benefits, such as inflation protection, often severely reduce the amount of income you will receive and limit their value.

The Fixed Annuity

Ever since a Pennsylvania insurance company offered the first commercial contract in 1912, fixed annuities have provided a secure form of savings for millions of conservative investors.

In a fixed annuity, you have the option to make either a lump sum payment or in many cases fund the annuity with periodic payments. The insurance company will, in turn, pay a guaranteed fixed interest rate for a stated period, usually one to ten years, but it could be longer. At the end of the period, when the annuity matures, in most cases, they will automatically renew at a revised interest rate unless you withdraw or move the money. Rates of return will depend on current interest rates and reset when the annuity matures.

If you are familiar with CDs, fixed annuities work in essentially the same manner. They are both issued for a stated amount of time at a stated interest rate. In both cases, there will be a penalty for early withdrawal. In the case of the annuity, it will be a surrender charge, which will be based on a percentage of the current value of the annuity. Unlike the CD, the interest buildup in the annuity grows tax-deferred. Tax-deferral, however, comes at a price as any withdrawals from the annuity before age 59 ½ will incur an additional 10 percent penalty from the IRS.

A fixed annuity belongs to a class of annuities called *deferred annuities.* With deferred annuities, annuitization is deferred into the future, allowing the annuity to grow. Income from a fixed annuity is obtained via two general methods. First, you can receive payments of only the interest on a periodic basis, such as monthly or annually. Second, at some point in the future, the fixed annuity can be annuitized and income taken over the period of your choosing. Once you decide to annuitize the fixed annuity, you essentially turn the fixed annuity into an immediate annuity with all the advantages and disadvantages previously discussed.

The Fixed Index Annuity

The fixed index annuity, also known as the equity index annuity or just index annuity for short, is, in many ways, similar to the fixed annuity. Both offer tax-deferred growth, the potential for a lifetime income, and certain guarantees. However, unlike the fixed annuity, the index annuity does not have a fixed maturity or interest rate.

In an index annuity, your money can earn either an annual rate of interest that is guaranteed by the insurance company or an interest rate based on the growth of some external index. These indices may include the S&P, Dow Jones, or NASDAQ, among others. It is important to note that while an external market index may affect your contract value, the contract does not directly invest your money in shares of stocks, bonds, or any other market investment.

Interest earned on the annuity is calculated annually and based on the performance of the index and the crediting method chosen, adjusted for any interest rate caps, participation percentage or rates, and spreads. The crediting method is how the index return will be calculated. Some of the more popular crediting methods are annual point-to-point, which compares the beginning and ending value of the chosen index for the year, and the monthly average or monthly sum methods, which use monthly values of the index in different ways to calculate your return. Crediting methods available will vary from contract to contract and carrier to carrier.

In most cases, you will not be credited with the entire gain in the index. Don't be misled into thinking you can. In most contracts, the interest will be calculated and credited annually on the anniversary date of the contract. If the annual calculation is positive, you will get interest credited to your account. However, if the calculation is negative, you lose nothing. You simply get no interest for the year. This annual reset feature is a key selling point with index annuities and what makes them unique. You cannot lose money, no matter how much the market may be down unless you surrender the contract during the surrender period.

Also, the ending index values for the contract year becomes the beginning values for the following year. This means that if there is a loss in an index for a given year, the index does not have to recover that loss for you to profit the following year.

Think about what that would have meant after 2008. When the index is up, you may have a gain - depending on possible spreads, when the index is down, you simply stay flat.

Exhibit 11.1 Example of the Growth of a Fixed Index Annuity

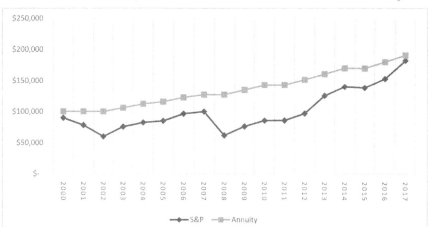

Illustration shows the growth of the S&P 500 Index vs. a hypothetical Fixed Index Annuity purchased Jan. 1, 2000. Example assumes a 1-year S&P point-to-point crediting with a 6% cap and does not represent a specific product for sale.

Like most other annuities, the interest buildup in the contract grows tax deferred until you begin withdrawals and contain death benefits payable to your beneficiaries in the case of your death. Again, these benefits will vary greatly from contract to contract.

While most index annuities will have a surrender charge that can last from perhaps seven to ten years or more, most will let you withdraw up to ten percent per year without incurring a surrender charge. The surrender charge usually won't apply if the withdrawals are taken as part of an income rider or a required minimum distribution from a retirement account.

As with all these potential benefits and charges, it is imperative that you understand how each contract works.

Don't assume that any two contracts work the same, even those from the same -they usually don't.

Income from a fixed index annuity can take place in various ways, including annuitization, taking periodic partial withdrawals, or by the use of a lifetime income rider. The lifetime income rider is what makes the index annuity potentially a key component in your retirement income solution.

The lifetime income rider goes by many different names. In fact, each company may call it something else. What the rider does is provide for a lifetime income (may be either single-life or joint with a spouse) from the annuity, at some future date, **without annuitizing** the contract. Remember annuitization is one of the drawbacks of the immediate annuity. How it accomplishes this can be extremely complex. The biggest source of confusion and ultimately dissatisfaction with annuities is the misunderstanding of the different values an annuity purchaser sees in their statement. In essence, what's cash and what's not?

One thing to keep in mind is there are almost as many different income riders as there are annuity contracts. Also, each company will use different methodology and different terminology when it comes to their contracts and riders. The rider on the contract you may own, or are looking to purchase, will be different. It is imperative that you understand how any rider works and what it costs.

Four key components go into understanding an annuity with an income rider. First, as with all annuities, you have the cash or accumulation value. This is the true - cash you can spend - value of the annuity. Remember, the annuity will have a surrender charge, usually for the first seven to ten years or longer. Your statement will always contain the cash value net of any surrender charge. This is the only real cash number there is.

Second, there's the *income account value*. This will go by many names, and I think each company has their own. This value represents the value that will be used to calculate your lifetime income. The income account value is not cash, and you cannot take it in a lump sum. More on how this grows in a moment.

The key selling point in many of the contracts is the guaranteed growth of the income account value. These riders will have what's often called a roll-up rate. This is the third component. The roll-up rate is laid out in the contract when you purchase the annuity and is the rate that the income account is guaranteed to grow by every year. Be very careful; this is one of the places where those other guys talk about big returns. You may see roll-up rates of between four and seven percent.

The formula for the growth of the income account value will vary from contract to contract. What follows is a generic explanation.

Each year, the income account value will grow by the greater of the roll-up rate or the actual interest credit from the crediting method you chose. Just like the cash value of the annuity, the income account value will lock in at each year's value and is not subject to losses from down markets.

Now, you should see why the income account value is usually greater than the cash value. Even in years that you get no interest credit, the income account will still grow by the roll-up rate. The longer you have the contract, the bigger the potential difference between the cash value and the income account value may be. One note here: If you are looking at one of these riders, be sure to ask how long roll-up lasts. In many cases, it's only ten years but may be renewed for longer. You may have to take action.

Ultimately, the reason we would purchase an income rider is to get a guaranteed lifetime income. This is where the fourth component, the withdrawal factor or withdrawal percentage, comes in. When you're ready to begin taking lifetime income from the annuity, your income account value will be multiplied by the withdrawal factor to arrive at your annual income number. This is your paycheck.

Here's another place where the sales guys talk about huge returns. The withdrawal rates, which like the roll-up rate are part of the contract, are most often presented in 5 or 10 year bands. For instance, a 65-year-old may have a withdrawal rate of 5 percent, whereas if you wait until 80 to begin withdrawals, that rate could go up to as high as 7 percent. They may push the 7 percent rate, but that won't do you much good if you want income at 65. This is only an illustration, but I hope you get the point.

Exhibit 11.2   Example of Annuity Withdrawal Bands

Age	Single Payment	Joint Payment
59.5 - 64	4.50%	4.00%
65 - 69	5.00%	4.50%
70 - 74	5.50%	5.00%
75 - 79	6.00%	5.50%
80 - 84	6.50%	6.00%
85 - 89	7.00%	6.50%
90+	7.50%	7.00%

Above example is for illustration purposes only.

Now, I hope you're not totally confused at this point. Let me simplify the whole subject. You want income. The important thing for you and the only number that really matters is the annual income. Many annuity guys will try to sell you on the growth of the income account value but ignore an extremely low withdrawal percentage. You can eliminate all the confusion by just comparing the projected income value for each annuity - but be careful.

Annuities are usually sold using an analysis called an illustration. This is a report that will show both the guaranteed values of the annuity and the lifetime income rider over time, along with projected or illustrated values based on historical, back-tested performance. Be very careful here. The annuity guys will point you to the projected numbers to show how much your annuity and rider will be worth. Make sure you start with the guaranteed values and work up from there. Chances are you'll wind up with something in between the guaranteed and illustrated values.

And last, understand whether your income will have some sort of growth potential or if it's fixed. If there is a potential for an income increase, you need to understand how it works and how likely you are to get an increase. I have reviewed many annuities that advertise an increasing income. In all but a few cases, the increase, while possible, is highly unlikely to occur.

Many annuity jockeys use the relatively high first- year payment of a fixed lifetime income as a selling point. Remember, the number one financial risk in retirement is ignoring the effect of inflation. While a big income number year one may look good, if it doesn't grow, you may be in trouble down the road unless inflation was taken into account in your financial plan.

Index annuities can protect from loss, provide indexed interest potential, tax deferral, and as you will see, some pretty valuable ways to guarantee income for life. So what's the problem?

The problem is in the way some annuity jockeys are positioning and selling these products. Fixed index annuities were never meant to compete with stock index returns. Contrary to what you may be told, they are not growth products. Sales guys that sell these as *investment killers* and try to get you to put all your money in these products as protection from stock market volatility are not telling you the entire story.

On its own, the fixed index annuity can potentially provide a return that is greater than other instruments with similar risk profiles. This would include things like CDs, T-Bills, and fixed annuities. What makes the index annuity an appealing choice as part of your retirement income plan is the ability, through the use of a lifetime income rider, to receive a guaranteed lifetime income without having to annuitize the contract. This means that you won't lose control of your money, as is the case if you annuitize a contract and one of the big negatives the annuity haters out there constantly bring up.

Hopefully, the preceding discussion didn't make your eyes glaze over and your head hurt. As I've said, annuities can be extremely complex financial products with a bunch of moving parts, often sold by those that would be better suited selling used cars. They are, however, well worth the effort to understand as they can be a key player in your retirement income solution.

While purchasing an annuity with a lifetime income rider may sound like a daunting task, it isn't. Everything we've discussed here should work hand-in-hand with your financial plan and should be easy to understand if properly explained. Perhaps that's the key. If you don't understand, don't sign a thing. The key is to work with a financial professional and not an annuity jockey. Hopefully, by now, you know the difference.

The Variable Annuity

The Variable Annuity, or VA, is undoubtedly the most complex and expensive product in the annuity family. Whereas the other types of annuities, immediate, fixed, and fixed index, are all considered insurance products, the variable annuity is a combination insurance product and security product. As such, anyone who offers a variable annuity for sale must be both life insurance and securities licensed, whereas only a life insurance license is needed to offer the other types of annuities for sale.

A variable annuity is also, in many ways, similar to a garden variety fixed annuity. Both offer tax-deferred growth, the potential for a lifetime income, and certain guarantees.

However, like the index annuity, the VA does not have a fixed maturity or interest rate.

The biggest difference, and what makes the VA a unique product, is that the premium deposited into the annuity can be invested into stock and bond subaccounts. The rate of return on a VA is based on the investment performance of these subaccounts. Since these subaccounts are invested directly into market instruments, their value, and subsequently the value of your annuity, can fluctuate on a daily basis.

While VAs have the opportunity to provide good returns due to their investments, they are also the riskiest annuity you can purchase. Unlike most other annuity products, your premium investment and any growth do not lock in, as is the case with the index annuity. VAs also have lifetime income riders available. The gains in the income account value will often lock in at high-water marks at periods that vary among the different annuities.

Conventional wisdom would say that VAs are appropriate for someone who wants or needs a higher return than can be obtained by a fixed or fixed index annuity, or someone who has a higher risk tolerance. It is my experience that this is not how they're sold. Many brokers sell VAs as a lower risk alternative to the stock market for those that are less tolerant of market risk. These brokers usually explain that the protection of the various riders that can be attached to the contract lessen the risk, while making market returns available. I'm not sure this wisdom is sound.

Besides the market risk, which means no principal protection, the biggest drawback of VAs are the fees. Inside the VA, you will pay many different fees: some disclosed, some hard to find, and some that are just hidden. These fees include an administrative fee, mortality and expense fee, rider charges, fees for management of the subaccounts, and transaction fees in the subaccounts - a fee you will never see. Also, some contracts will charge a fee for portfolio rebalancing and other assorted stuff. I regularly review VAs that have total expenses greater than five percent per year, and I've seen a few that can run as much as eight percent. Also, as in many annuities, a declining surrender charge may apply for the first seven to ten years.

If you compare the return you are likely to get in the sub-accounts and subtract the fees, what's left may not seem like it is worth the risk to principal.

Overall, the reason to purchase a VA is the benefits it may offer above and beyond the growth potential. These benefits, which vary greatly among contracts, are usually available by contract rider, at an additional cost. Once again, this is where current interest rates, market conditions, and the insurer's appetite for risk come into play. They will directly impact the benefits and the cost of those benefits in the contracts.

VAs have changed tremendously since the financial crisis of 2008. In my opinion, changes to the products due to lower interest rates and a lower tolerance for risk by the insurers have made them more expensive and far less appealing and useful to the consumer.

Variable Annuities are extremely confusing to the consumer. In almost every case, when I review a VA that someone purchased, they have no idea how it works, the risk they are taking, or how much the VA costs them. In more cases than I can count, the reason the annuity was purchased was that they were told *the value was guaranteed to double in x years.* Of course, this is not true and only referring to the income account value or equivalent.

While Variable Annuities may be suitable for some, under the right conditions, there are likely better, less complex, less risky, and less costly options. I look at VAs as multitaskers that don't perform either function - insurance or investment - very well. Perhaps the biggest issue with VAs, just as with the index annuity, is the sales tactics and lack of knowledge of many of those who sell them.

The debate over annuities will probably never end. With the possible exception of the variable annuity, annuities can play a key role in the income portion of your retirement income solution. As with many other items I've discussed in these chapters, it's important to educate yourself about the subject, ask questions, don't be a bobblehead, and find the right financial professional that will provide a solution, not sell you a used car.

CHAPTER 12

Investing: You're Probably Doing It Wrong

Successful investing requires much more than purchasing a bunch of mutual funds based on an allocation derived from some outdated rule of thumb, but that's exactly what many individual investors do. Whether they invest themselves or enlist the services of a broker, the average investor ends up using the same products and buying into the same tactics.

There's a big problem with this practice - actually, there are many. Investors continually follow the pattern of searching for the latest can't-miss product, mutual fund, or stock because they wrongfully believe that's what they're supposed to do, and all they can do. The financial firms and media spend tremendous amounts of time and money to ensure that your focus is right where they want it to be; on their products and services. Welcome to the expensive, generic world of retail investing, where most investors are stuck, unaware that there's a better way.

The products and tactics used by the masses haven't changed much, even as better ways to invest have emerged. While a comprehensive review of all the products and tactics used by the average investor would take too long to have any value, I will show how some of the most commonly used may be putting your financial success at risk. This will certainly challenge some of the long-held beliefs you have about the market and investing.

While the masses are chasing the next big thing, many wealthy investors I have met, are focusing on something different: their goals. With the help and guidance of their investment advisors, high net worth families understand the reason they invest, and by now so should you.

Whether you're in the accumulation phase building your nest egg or investing the growth component of your retirement income solution, how you invest and who you invest with will be critical to your success. As I will show, it is possible for you to manage your investments like the wealthy and no longer be an average investor.

First, allow me a few moments to settle the debate over active versus passive investing, as I promised earlier. This debate highlights some of the key issues with the current thinking in investing.

The Active vs. Passive Debate

In 1976, John Bogle and the Vanguard Group launched the first retail index fund, the Vanguard 500 Index. Since then, the debate over active versus passive investing has become a topic of never-ending debate.

The financial media, investment managers, advisors, and many individual investors have very strong opinions on the subject. The debate centers around which method of investing provides superior returns for investors over the long run. As is the case with many of the debates in the financial world, the active versus passive debate is presented as an either/or decision. You're either a passive investor or an active investor, but you can't be both. I'm not sure who makes these rules, but once again I need to settle the debate.

For those of you who may not know what I'm talking about, here's a quick primer on the topic.

While passive investing can take many forms, it's most often associated with index investing. For example, the

Vanguard 500 Index contains only the 500 stocks in the S&P 500 index. There are no trading decisions to make since the only time there should be trading in the fund is when companies are added or removed from the index.

The theory - in a nutshell—behind passive investing is that it's impossible to beat the market in the long run and by limiting the amount of trading in an account and thus reducing costs and fees, the investor will profit. Simply buy the index and hold on tight.

The major question, and one often ignored, is which index? The free-advice crowd often steers its listeners into the Vanguard 500 Index. However, the S&P 500 only includes 500 large cap stocks. Does it make sense that all your money should be in one type of stock? What about small-cap, mid-cap, international, fixed income, and the many other indices and sectors available for the passive investor?

Active investing entails a portfolio manager making buy and sell decisions that are based on some model, strategy, or forecast. The goal of many actively managed investments is to take advantage of short or long-term price fluctuations in the market, or usually a piece of the market or sector to outperform their benchmark index. Benchmarks can be very complex and may have nothing to do with the more common indices, such as the S&P 500. Most mutual funds are actively managed.

Some actively managed investments are designed specifically to hedge or manage risk. Risk managed strategies are not designed to beat the market as we commonly think of it but to protect against adverse market moves or other events that may prove detrimental to your net worth.

The trading activity of actively managed funds and the need for portfolio managers, analysts, and associated back-office staff means that the trading costs and fees of active management will be higher than that of passive investments. This is obviously seen as a negative and one of the rallying cries of the passive advocates.

The active versus passive debate always heats up during periods of market extremes. The debate is a function of our collectively short memories and an either/or mentality pushed on us by those that advocate one theory or the other. Beating the market is hard: But is that your goal?

When markets are good, it's hard not to get caught up in the hype and hysteria. In periods where the market is rising almost daily, and volatility is low - think 2017 - passive investing is hard to beat. You get market returns - and market risk - at a very low cost.

It's much harder, in times like this, for active managers to add value, especially given the added cost. Also, since most indices are doing well during this period, the choice of which index to choose doesn't seem all that important. With the help of the financial media and pundits, we tend to forget about risk when times are good. Remember the *New Economy* touted by the financial pundits during the dot-com boom?

What about when times are not so great? Add a little volatility to the party, an ugly correction, or worse, a bear market, and the passively managed portfolio might get a bit uncomfortable. The dot-com bust and the financial crisis of 2008-2009 weren't fun times.

With passive investing, there is no market risk control. Your returns and risk are at the mercy of the market. We must manage risk!

One of the biggest misconceptions is that the goal of active management is simply to beat the market. For many active managers, the goal is to provide superior risk-adjusted returns. I'll get deeper into this subject in chapter 14.

Unlike passive managers, who have no discretion in their investment choices, active managers can adjust their portfolios as market forecasts and conditions dictate. While this may, under certain conditions, limit some upside in the portfolio, it can also protect the downside making some active management well worth the cost.

The passive versus active debate centers around market conditions of the recent past. It's easy to look back in time and determine which strategy would have provided better returns. It's not so easy to see into the future

The choice of investment strategies, like most other financial issues, is NOT and should NOT be an either/ or decision. No single investment strategy can succeed in all market conditions. A properly constructed portfolio should be designed to achieve your goals and objectives and should combine the low-cost market returns of passive investing and the risk management capabilities of actively managed strategies. Always remember, your investment goals are much more complex than simply to beat the market.

Retail Investing: For the Masses

Many investors have no idea that there's a problem with the way they invest. They're not aware that the products they invest in may be expensive, the advice suspect, and many of the assumptions dangerous. If this is you, it's not your fault. Most investors don't know they have a choice.

The purpose of the retail financial industry is to make money for the industry, not for you. In any given transaction, there are multiple layers of individuals and firms with their hands in your pocket. They do not exist to help you; they exist to make a profit at your expense.

Remember, as of the writing of this book, the brokers that sell you products, call you with the latest hot stock tip or the trading recommendations of their *Senior Analyst,* or sell you a portfolio of mutual funds do not work for you. They don't need to work in your best interest and their advice, if that's what you call it, may be geared toward nothing more than making sales and generating commissions. They work for their firm, not you. They are not bound to a fiduciary standard. Sorry, but that's the way it works. Even if the SEC enacts a *best interest rule,* it may not significantly change these facts.

It is imperative that you understand this point: **The retail financial industry does not exist to ensure your financial success. It exists to generate a profit, and you are the source of that profit.**

The average investor is stuck in the retail world because he doesn't know there's a choice. There is.

Mutual Funds: Are They the Right Investment Choice For You?

Mutual funds are the predominant investment tool of the retail investor. As of December 31, 2016, American households held 89 percent of the $16.3 trillion invested in U.S. mutual funds.[27]

Advertised as an inexpensive way to invest your money, they have become the primary tool of the retail investor and the darling of the do-it-yourself, free-advice crowd. For a segment of the population, mutual funds are an excellent investment choice. They offer the retail investor access to professional portfolio management, a simple way to diversify, liquidity, and in many cases, for only $50 an individual can begin to invest for their future. While they may seem like a good investment vehicle, and they often are, I find few investors who are aware of their true cost and inefficiencies.

Mutual funds are pooled investments. With pooled investments you have no control over any of the activity in the fund or investment. The only things you can control are which funds to buy and sell (including possibly share class), how much, and when. This means that once you purchase shares in a mutual fund you are subject to the rules and regulations that govern these instruments. This can be a good thing for many investors who are *forced*, to give up the investment decisions to a professional manager. It can also be a bad thing, subjecting investors to potential inefficiencies in the way the mutual fund structure operates.

For example, mutual funds are required to distribute realized capital gains and income, usually in the form of dividends, to the fund's shareholders. Often, the mutual fund holds shares that had appreciated over many years, well before you owned your shares in the fund. Even if you didn't participate in the gain of individual stocks, you would have a tax due on any appreciated stocks that the manager sells either from a change to the portfolio or from redemptions of existing shareholders. In a taxable account this cost can add up (it should not be a concern in a non-taxable or tax-deferred account). While you may not think this is a big issue, think back to 2008. Many investors were shocked when, during the financial meltdown that saw their portfolios take a sizable hit, they received an IRS form 1099 from their broker for the income they received during the year.

This is just one example. The point here is that while mutual funds may be an excellent choice for many investors and savers just starting out, there may be better portfolio vehicles for the investor who wants more control over the tax and allocation decisions of their portfolios. Very often, you do have a choice.

What Is the Real Cost of Your Investment?

One of the rallying cries of the financial gurus is that the fees charged by an investment advisor do little more than reduce the return on your assets. There have been countless articles written that outline the cost of financial advice, most often over the time you are saving for retirement. Why use an advisor when you can invest in no-load mutual funds? They make it seem like no-load funds are free. Nothing could be further from the truth. In fact, in many cases, mutual funds can be significantly more expensive to an investor than working with, and gaining the value of a relationship with, an investment advisor.

Do you have any idea how much your investments are costing? No, no you don't. The total cost of many investment vehicles is very difficult, if at all possible, to discover. Even if you read and can understand the prospectus - which let's face it, few do - you would need to hire a forensic accountant to get close to the total costs you incur. But does understanding the detailed cost of your investment even matter?

While a detailed, math-packed, discussion of the calculation and understanding of all the costs associated with any investment vehicle is beyond the scope of this book – and probably your desire to read - I think it's important to understand the various components of cost so you can make a meaningful comparison between investments or strategies without having to rely on the marketing propaganda you may hear. For simplicity sake, let's break those costs down into three categories: Direct costs, *hidden* costs, and ancillary costs and understand the importance – or lack of importance - of each.

First, let's look at direct costs. These are the costs and fees that are associated with the purchase, sale, or holding of an investment or account. These costs – if they exist - are usually paid directly by the investor in some fashion. They may come out of your account, or perhaps as a reduction in the amount invested or sold. In certain cases, the fees may even be paid from other accounts not related to the investment. They should be fully visible (somewhere) on an account statement. Direct costs would include items such as commissions, advisory and management fees, and account fees, among others.

It is vitally important for an investor to understand the direct costs they are paying. Generally, these costs will not be included in the published returns of an investment. While some investment types will publish returns net of these fees (management/advisory), since the fees may vary by investor, these published returns will only be a periodic indication and not directly relate to you. Also, items such as commissions and account fees can vary greatly between brokers. In order to understand the true cost and return of an investment you must understand if and how direct costs are included in any return calculations.

Next, we have the hidden costs. I refer to them as hidden only because they generally do not show up on a statement.

These are the internal costs for operating the investment. They might include items such as expenses, trading costs inside the investment, marketing, distribution, and, among other things, the cost of insurance for fixed insurance products. While many of these costs and fees will be disclosed in the prospectus, or contract in the case of an insurance product, they are not easily visible to the investor as they do not show up on their statement.

Generally, these hidden costs and fees will already be included in the price and subsequent performance of the investment – such as mutual funds. That means that regardless of the level of these costs inside a particular investment, the published returns of two similar investments can be compared. While hidden costs should not be ignored in a comparison between investments, of the three types of costs and fees I am discussing, they are certainly the least important for the individual investor.

Last, we have what I call the ancillary costs. These are items that are associated with owning the investment but perhaps not attached to the investment. Included here are items such as the tax treatment and any operational inefficiencies of the vehicle.

As previously discussed, when a mutual fund distributes capital gains and dividends in the fund, you are left with a tax liability. Remember, even if you didn't participate in the gain of individual stocks, you would have a tax due on any appreciated stocks the manager sells.

Many investors don't realize that a dividend distribution will lower the price of the fund in the same way that the price of a stock is reduced when a dividend is paid. Let's use a simple example (the values are for illustrative purposes only) of a mutual fund that you purchase 100 shares of at $25/share for an investment of $2,500. During the year, distributions are made to the shareholders of $5/share. After the distributions (assuming they happen at one time), the new share price is $20/share. Assuming you are reinvesting your dividends back into the fund, as many mutual fund investors do, you now own 125 shares at a price of $20/share, but you have a tax liability on the $500 in reportable distributions. The tax liability is your cost.

Different investment types may have different ancillary costs. It is up to the investor to understand these costs, their effect on their wallet, and how they may differ between investment choices.

Understanding what you are paying for an investment is required if you are to understand the real rate-of-return on the investment or if you are trying to compare different investments, methodologies or strategies. If you recall from chapter five, calculating the rate-of-return on an investment is more involved than just comparing the purchase and sale price. While the price of the investment should include all the hidden costs and fees, you must include all the direct costs incurred in buying, holding, and selling the investment as well as adjusting for taxes.

Fees, costs, and expenses are an often-discussed, sometimes hotly debated topic in the financial world. At the writing of this book there appears to be a price war among some of the bigger brokerages to slash prices on many products to nothing. While this may seem like a good thing, you must be very careful making judgement based on price alone. While this may be the mantra of every sales guy ever, it is, none-the-less, true; *price - or cost – is only an issue in the absence of value.* As I've previously stated, cheap doesn't necessarily mean good.

To sum up this extremely simplified discussion of a complex topic, when looking at the performance of your investments or making comparisons among investments, control your direct costs where you can, understand the impact of your ancillary costs, and don't sweat what's already accounted for in the price. And, never, ever forget about risk!

Nontraded Instruments

While I hope you've learned quite a bit from this book, if there's only one lesson that you take away, let it be that you will NEVER invest in a product that you don't fully understand. That would eliminate many of the problems I see when I meet a new family and certainly eliminate the problems with nontraded instruments.

Retail brokers love nontraded instruments. They sound sexy when they explain them to an unsuspecting and trusting client and up until recently commanded an extremely high commission. Thankfully, new regulations are making these investments a little less profitable for the brokers to dump on unsuspecting investors.

Nontraded investments are a class of investments that do not trade on an exchange and as such are not liquid. The most common of these is the REIT or real estate investment trust. Nontraded investments are also available in business development corporations (BDCs), oil wells (usually in the form of a partnership), and hedge funds, among others. While they all work a bit differently, the major issues cut through them all.

In the case of the REITs or BDCs, the selling point is the dividend. Many of these investments will pay an annual dividend of 7 percent or more. This is extremely attractive for an individual looking for income with interest rates at very low levels. This income comes with a catch.

Nontraded means that these instruments are not traded on an exchange. Investments in nontraded investments are extremely illiquid, meaning you cannot easily get your money back if you need to. In many cases, if you want or need your money, you are required to make a formal request - usually available only once a quarter - that may or may not be accepted.

As with most of the products sold by the retail brokers, these nontraded investments are, in my opinion, not designed to make you money. If you read the prospectus for one of these, you will see the extremely high fees that are a product of multiple levels of management. There's a lot of hands in your pocket. Although these investments are required to pay 90 percent of profits back to the investors, with all the different parties taking a piece, there may not be much left.

The biggest risk and one the brokers certainly don't stress is that there is a chance that you will NEVER get your money back. In the case of REITs and BDCs, the objective is what's called a liquidity event. This is where the investment will go public (although there are other liquidity events) and the investors can get their money, usually with a nice profit. Not all of these investments will have a liquidity event. Like any business, some just go broke with no way for investors to recover their investment.

The list of major issues with these investments is long, and I've only scratched the surface. With the lack of liquidity and high risk to your principal, I can't think of a situation where nontraded investments are appropriate for any investor, regardless of net worth.

My rule with investing is simple. Except for insurance products, I will never invest a family's assets in anything that can't be sold with the click of a mouse! In the case of the asset classes covered by the non- traded investments, there are listed alternatives available that are easily, and quickly, bought and sold.

In my opinion, nontraded investments are not worth the risk. If people were forced to read the prospectus and be tested on its contents before investing, it is doubtful anyone would take the risk.

Bad things happen when you don't take the time to understand the products or investments you're being sold. If you're not willing to read and understand a prospectus on a complex investment, and who does, maybe it's not a good investment for you. Remember, the people who sell this stuff are sales guys who don't work for you. Their job is to sell, and many of them are really good at it.

While there are many more products I can go over, the analysis would be the same. The products sold by the retail brokers are not as good as their sales pitch makes them seem. What should you expect? If you deal with a sales guy, you're going to get sold.

Flawed Tactics: Stocks, Bonds, and the 60/40 Portfolio

Assumptions are not the same as facts. Confusing the two can be dangerous. The most dangerous assumptions are those that are never questioned since it is assumed that they are not assumptions at all, but instead are a financial law. What would happen if one of these assumptions, the basis of much of the portfolio construction done by individuals and financial professionals, turned out not to be true?

As I've previously stated, diversification is one of the most misused and misunderstood words in the financial lexicon. The prevailing thought is that diversification in a portfolio is simply the percentage of stocks and bonds that are contained in the portfolio. We are taught and have come to accept that the 60/40 portfolio - 60 percent stocks/40 percent bonds - the benchmark for the moderate risk portfolio - is less risky than an 80/20 portfolio. Why is this true? It has to do with something called correlation.

In portfolio management, correlation refers to the degree to which two securities move in relation to each other. Correlation, or more accurately, the coefficient of correlation of any two securities has a value between -1, perfect negative correlation, and 1, perfect correlation.

When two securities are perfectly correlated, changes in the price of one security are perfectly mirrored in the other. Securities that are perfectly negatively correlated will move in the exact opposite direction. When two securities have a correlation coefficient of zero, their movement in relation to each other is random; they may move together or apart. To achieve a diversified portfolio, you would want assets that are as negatively correlated to each other as possible. This means that when some go up, others will go down.

This all seems to make sense. After all, stocks and bonds move in opposite directions, right? That's what most people seem to think (ask your stock guy his thoughts). In fact, that statement will always get someone's bobblehead shaking in agreement. There's only one problem: it's not necessarily true!

Actually, over time the correlation between stocks and bonds is more likely to be positive than negative. Since the late 90s, the stock/bond correlation has been negative; however, since 2015, it has been moving back toward zero. Before this recent period of negative correlation, the stock/bond correlation was positive for over 40 years.[28]

What does it mean for all the portfolios whose risk management (diversification) is based on a flawed premise? What happens to the risk of these portfolios as the stock/bond correlation moves to zero or even positive?

While an allocation to bonds can certainly be used as part of your asset allocation, other less or non-correlated asset classes should be included. These may include assets such as real estate, commodities, and private equity, among others. While once these alternative asset classes were reserved for the wealthy, they are all readily available through liquid instruments – the only way I will use them - that can be bought and sold with the click of a mouse. And don't forget about annuities, and as I will show in chapter 13, life insurance. The risk/return characteristics of these products, coupled with an interesting (non)correlation story, may make them an ideal addition to a portfolio.

The preceding was simplified for your consumption as diversification and portfolio construction are fairly complex and math-intensive subjects. My point, though, is simple. Conventional wisdom, however it comes about, is dangerous. Basing your investment decisions on it, especially when not true, can end badly without you ever seeing a problem coming.

I cannot fault individuals who fall into these traps. They know no better. However, financial professionals who subscribe to the conventional wisdom, such as the 4 percent rule, the stock/bond correlation myth, or many others I haven't mentioned, are either lacking in financial knowledge or just lazy. Neither is a good answer.

You've worked too hard to get to where you are. You deserve better. It's time for you to exit the retail investment world.

Investment Advisors: Bound to a Fiduciary Standard

As I discussed in chapter 3, there are big differences between brokers and investment advisors. Again, a broker is regulated by the Suitability Standard. This means that his recommendations need only be suitable for you - a pretty low ethical and regulatory hurdle. He does not work for you and is not required to work in your best interest. Given all that, I would have to assume that the only reason someone would work with a broker is that they don't know any better. Now you do.

An investment advisor, acting in that capacity, has a fiduciary duty to you. This means that their duty and loyalty are to you. They have a legal duty to act in your best interest. They work for you. The investment advisor relationship is seen by many as the gold-standard of financial advice.

Unlike the broker who is paid based on commission, which may give the broker incentive to over-trade your account, investment advisors are usually paid a fee based on a percentage of the assets under management. The incentive for the investment advisor is to grow your account, which will subsequently grow his fees. Most advisors have no incentive to trade accounts as they do not share in any trading revenue. All fees and costs associated with your relationship with an investment advisor should be clearly disclosed in an Investment Advisory Agreement and Investment Policy Statement.

In short, do you want to work for someone who is loyal to you or a company? While it seems like a simple choice - and it should be - it's important to understand that not all investment advisors are created equal. While they may all go by the investment advisor title, the service they provide can be dramatically different.

Note: For the sake of this discussion, I will focus only on the investment-related activities of the advisor. This will be just one piece of the puzzle that will go into choosing the right advisor for your needs. Other ancillary services you'll require, such as financial planning, estate planning, etc., will also need to be analyzed.

The primary role of an investment advisor is to manage your investments. They accomplish this by creating and managing portfolios to satisfy a specific need or risk profile. One of the biggest differences between investment advisors will be their investment methodology.

While there are many different methodologies that an investment advisor can use to create portfolios, they primarily fall into five categories. It's important that you understand the different methodologies to ensure that the investment advisor you're working with is investing your money in a way that meets your requirements and expectations. Once again, you must understand what you're getting before you commit your money. Let's take a look at the first four:

- **Stock pickers and system traders:** These advisors create portfolios for clients by picking individual investments using either fundamental or technical analysis.

- **Mutual funds or other pooled investments:** Many advisors use mutual funds to create portfolios for clients. Some of the larger firms will use proprietary pooled investments, usually one for each risk tolerance level, to manage the accounts of clients under an asset threshold which may be $1 million to $5 million.

- **Specialty Advisors:** These are investment advisors who focus on a narrow segment of the market, managing portfolios where specialized knowledge is needed.

These may include bonds, or more specifically a sub-set of bonds such as municipal bonds. Other specialties may include options, dividend-paying stocks, or a focus on a particular sector of the market.

- **Money Managers:** Some firms are built around offer-ing clients a select group of portfolios they manage in-house. Instead of customizing portfolios for clients, these firms design and manage a limited number of portfolios that are available for investors. These portfolios may be differentiated by risk tolerance level, market capitaliza-tion, market sector, or some other criteria.

Your situation may require the need for more than one of these advisors. For instance, if a large part of your wealth is tied up in company stock, you may need an investment advi-sor that specializes in stock option strategies to protect the value of that stock. You may also have other portfolio needs that must be addressed, requiring a different advisor using a different methodology. Using multiple investment advisors can be inefficient and hard to manage for all but the uber-wealthy. What's needed is an investment advisor who has access to portfolio managers that can meet all your portfolio needs.

Institutional-Level Asset Management: The Way the Wealthy Invest

Back in my days at Revlon, I was fortunate to be able to do work for some of the other companies owned by Ron Perel-man. That's how I got involved with Coleman and ultimately Sunbeam. One of my responsibilities at this time was manag-ing the combined pensions of all his companies. This was my introduction to institutional asset management.

Managing a pension of that size had nothing to do with sitting in front of a screen and picking stocks. We were not concerned with the micromanagement of individual invest-ments as many are on the personal side. The process started, together with the pension committee, by creating an asset allocation strategy for all the pension assets. Without going into all the details, the asset allocation was designed to achieve a certain level of risk and a target expected return.

Inside of Perelman's organization were some of the most brilliant financial minds I've had the pleasure to associate with - this was the committee.

Once the allocation was set, a pension consulting firm would identify the top managers in that asset class and do the appropriate due diligence. Then, along with the Treasurer of Revlon and the pension consultant, I would interview the finalists and make a recommendation to the committee. The end result, which might take months, would be the hiring of an asset manager for a specific asset class.

On an ongoing basis, my job was to manage the managers. It was my responsibility to ensure that the managers we hired continued to perform in the top quartile and adhere to their mandate of investing in the asset class for which they were hired. I always needed to be on the lookout for any red flags that would signal potential trouble. It was my job to ensure there would be no surprises that would jeopardize these assets. Let's face it, the last thing I ever wanted to do was go before the committee with bad news I should have seen coming!

This process made sense: set an asset allocation based on goals, hire the best managers for each part of the allocation, and let the managers do what they do best. This is the method used by pensions, large institutions, endowments, and the wealthy. Why shouldn't your assets be managed the same way?

Institutional-level asset management is the final methodology. Once reserved for the wealthy, today, with the aid of technology, investment advisors can manage your assets in the same manner that the assets of pensions and other large institutions are managed.

Working with an advisor who takes a highly consultative approach, your goals are established, and an asset allocation is created. Your assets are held in separate accounts that are supervised by third-party custodians. With the assistance of your advisor, your assets are managed directly in your account by the institutional-level money managers, following the asset allocation created by you and your advisor. These are not pooled investments, like mutual funds. The individual securities are registered in your name and held in your account.

In many cases, these investment advisors will have access to managers that can fill any portfolio need you might have. Instead of a generic portfolio, you are now able to have a portfolio that is designed to your specific needs at a cost that's probably much lower than you're paying for your retail mutual funds.

Hopefully, this chapter will entice you to take out those investment statements you haven't reviewed in a while and take a good look at how your hard-earned assets are being invested. If you're stuck in the expensive, generic world of retail investing, you now know that there's a better way.

CHAPTER 13

Life Insurance: The Swiss Army Knife of Financial Products

Properly used, life insurance may be one of the most versatile products in your financial arsenal. However, like annuities, it's not well understood, subject to questionable selling techniques, and the subject of derision and misinformation from many in the investment community since it funnels funds away from their control.

Life insurance, or more specifically, cash value life insurance, can play a much bigger role in a financial plan than providing a death benefit for its policyholders. Properly structured, cash value life insurance can be used to fund long-term care or chronic care needs, be used to provide a tax-advantaged source of income, maximize pension benefits, fund college, and many others.

In this chapter, I will give an overview of some of the many ways that life insurance can be used for both protection and as an asset class capable of providing both income and growth. It must be noted that these strategies, while powerful, are not suitable for every investor. Executing these strategies will take a combination of good health at the time of execution, sufficient assets to purchase the policy (without neglecting other parts of your plan), and an advisor knowledgeable in the field and capable of providing solutions from various carriers.

Before I begin, let's look at the various types of cash value life insurance and what makes it such a powerful financial asset.

Cash Value Life Insurance

There are various types of cash value life insurance, including whole life, variable universal life (VUL), index universal life (IUL), and current assumption universal life (UL). All are forms of permanent insurance, meaning that if the premiums are paid, the death benefit is guaranteed. All these policies will accumulate cash that can be used by the policyholder.

Since the main purpose of life insurance is to protect surviving family members, life insurance has been granted preferential tax treatment by the IRS. The tax benefits include:

- Income tax-free death benefit under most conditions
- Tax-deferred cash accumulation inside the policy
- Ability to access cash from the policy using tax- free policy loans

The tax benefits provide another way for policyholders to grow and protect their accumulating wealth, as well as allow greater flexibility with the use of other assets in retirement. Also, except for VUL, life insurance can provide an asset in your portfolio that is non-correlated to the stock market.

One of the biggest differences between the various policy types is the way the cash value is generated. The cash value in VUL and IUL policies grows in essentially the same way the cash value grows in their annuity counterparts. The IUL cash value will be tied to the annual performance of an index such as the S&P 500, usually subject to a cap, with the same downside protection guarantees, meaning your cash value, once credited, can never decrease. The cash in a VUL is invested in separate accounts containing stock and bond market investments identical to variable annuities. As such, while VUL has the largest growth potential, the cash balance is subject to market risk with no protection from loss.

In a UL policy, the cash left over after the cost of insurance and fees is credited with a rate of interest which will vary based on the insurance company's investment experience. A guaranteed minimum interest rate is included in the policy.

Whole life insurance comes in two flavors - participating and nonparticipating. Both types will accumulate interest in a manner similar to the method used for UL. The difference between nonparticipating and participating whole life is that participating whole life policies pay a dividend to the policyholders on an annual basis. Payment of dividends is not guaranteed; however, many highly rated, reputable insurance companies have been paying their dividends, without interruption, for well over 100 years. Dividends have been paid continually by these companies through the Depression, World Wars, and various periods of market and economic turmoil.

You have a choice as to what to do with your dividends in a participating whole life policy. They can be used to purchase paid-up additions (PUA), which are small pieces of paid-up insurance that will accumulate cash and dividends and increase the total death benefit. Other choices for your dividends include purchasing additional term insurance, they may be left to accumulate interest, used to reduce or make premium payments, reduce an existing policy loan, or simply be paid to you in cash. Your choice of how to apply the dividend can usually be changed on an annual basis as your needs change.

Other than the method by which the cash balance grows, the biggest difference between the various forms of universal life and whole life is in the payment of premium. Whole life policies have a guaranteed level premium that is contractually guaranteed never to change. In contrast, one of the features of universal life policies is a flexible payment of premiums. The policyholder can vary the amount placed in the policy each year - funding less in some years and funding the maximum in other years, based on the design of the policy. This flexibility allows for putting much more cash into the policy. The maximum amount will be determined by IRS guidelines based on the policy's death benefit.

A properly constructed life insurance strategy can have far-reaching benefits in your financial plan. It is a very versatile risk management tool. While each type has its advantages and disadvantages, I have trouble recommending VUL for any of the strategies I will outline below.

As a risk management tool, VUL falls short. Extremely high expenses, like in the variable annuity, combined with no guarantees on the cash balance, make its value as a risk management tool questionable. Like its cousin, the variable annuity, variable universal life is a multitasker that is neither a good insurance policy nor a good investment vehicle. If your only goal is death benefit, there are much better, less expensive ways to achieve your goal.

Life and Legacy Planning

Let's start with the two most common uses for permanent insurance in retirement: providing financial security for a spouse and providing for future generations.

Many families I meet initially balk at discussing life insurance. They assume that by the time they get to retirement age - assuming the kids and house are all taken care of - they won't need life insurance since the loss of income from the loss of a spouse will be offset by the reduction in costs. Unfortunately, this is seldom the case.

When one spouse passes away during retirement, there are losses in income that often go unplanned. At the very least, one Social Security will be lost. Also, there may be a loss of pension income from the deceased spouse. While this loss of income should have been covered in your financial plan, funding the income reduction through the addition of life insurance will ensure the surviving spouse can maintain their standard of living throughout retirement. The emotional strain of losing a spouse need not be compounded by the additional emotional turmoil created by worrying about money.

For many families, leaving a legacy to younger generations is not just a desire but a duty. As such, many families will spend as little as possible in retirement, so they can pass the most money on to their heirs upon their deaths. I have seen couples who have a substantial nest egg live at a poverty-like level for fear of not being able to fund their legacy.

In this instance, life insurance in an amount which will fund the legacy will act as a permission slip for the family to enjoy their retirement. Once the insurance is funded, the legacy is guaranteed, and the family can enjoy retirement safe in the knowledge that their legacy will be passed to future generations. Now, let's look at some other uses for permanent life insurance that you may not be aware of.

Long-Term Care

As I previously discussed, a large percentage of Americans will require some form of long-term care at some point in their lives. As the need for long-term care insurance (LTCI) increases, so does the cost. According to a study by the Society of Actuaries, rate increases approved by regulators have averaged more than 20 percent in recent years.[29]

Besides the increasing cost, LTCI has a few other drawbacks. The first of these is that the premiums paid for LTCI are not guaranteed. This means that your annual cost can rise (significantly) as you age. Also, the policies have no cash value or death benefit, meaning that they are a use it or lose it policy, like your auto or homeowner's insurance. Families can pay premiums for many years and pass away without using the coverage, not being able to recover any of the premium paid into the policy. I have seen firsthand where couples in their 90s have paid over $200,000 into LTCI that they will probably never use.

This may be a big part of the reason why only 12 percent of people in their late 50's and early 60s have purchased LTCI coverage.[30]

In response to these issues, many life insurance providers have created hybrid or combination life insurance/LTCI policies. These policies will often allow the policyholder to accelerate the death benefit if long-term care is needed. Other policies will combine both life and LTCI in the same policy, and others will use annuities.

These policies and their provisions vary widely among carriers. Once again, it is extremely important to understand the different policies so you can analyze the best option for your situation. This can only be done while working with an advisor who can show you policies of differing types from competing companies.

Properly structured, the premium payments in the life/LTCI policies will be guaranteed, meaning they can never increase. Also, if you never need long-term care, the death benefit will be available to pass to your heirs. You won't lose it if you don't use it.

Using Life Insurance as an Asset Class

While usually looked at as a protection asset, cash value life insurance can play an important role as an asset in your portfolio. According to Michael Finke, professor of personal financial planning at Texas Tech, the cash value in a whole life policy should provide more income, dollar-for-dollar, than bonds held in a taxable or tax-sheltered account. [31] Not too bad for a low risk, uncorrelated asset.

From an income perspective, the ability to access the cash value of the policy through tax-free loans can play a key role in your retirement income solution. First, policyholders can take periodic loans to create a monthly (or another period) stream of income payments. Since they are policy loans, the income is free from income tax. This strategy can be used to add retirement income and reduce taxable income, while giving you the ability to preserve other assets. Your advisor will be able to illustrate the amount you can safely take from the policy. When employing a loan strategy, it is imperative that the policy is reviewed annually. The risk of this strategy is that you take too much out of the policy, causing the policy to lapse and creating an adverse tax event.

Combining portfolio assets, annuities, and life insurance may enable a policyholder to use a larger withdrawal rate from the portfolio than might otherwise be prudent. To protect against sequence of returns and potentially depleting your account, loans from the policy can be used to fund income in years after a down market, allowing the portfolio assets time to recover.

This is just a quick overview of two of the ways life insurance can be used as a portfolio asset. There are others that can be deployed, depending on your situation. Much to the chagrin of the broker boys, allocating part of your assets to cash value life insurance may provide a better outcome than stocks and bonds alone.

Maximizing Your Pension Income

If you are one of the fortunate few who will receive pension benefits when you retire, you will need to choose your pension option—how you will take your benefit. Most people elect a joint payout with a spouse, usually with a 50 percent survivor benefit. This means that when the pension holder passes away, their spouse's income will be cut in half, creating a potential cash flow problem. Also, choosing a pension option with a survivor benefit will reduce the amount of your benefit while you're alive. Depending on the amount of your pension, the survivor benefit could cost hundreds of dollars per month.

Using permanent life insurance, you can maximize both the pension value and survivor benefit. By holding permanent life insurance, you may elect the higher single life payment. The death benefit will be available to provide the income needed by the surviving spouse, while the higher single life payment will provide more income to enjoy while you're alive.

College Planning

If you're the parent of a newborn or young child, you are no doubt thinking about how to save and pay for college. While this topic may be slightly outside of the focus of this book, it's important to include since saving and paying for college can often come at the expense of retirement savings.

Conventional wisdom and a lot of advertising would lead you to believe that 529 plans are the best and only way to save for college. Like every other financial decision, you should analyze its merits based on your individual situation. The benefits of a 529 plan will vary based on your state of residence.

The tax advantaged nature of cash-value life insurance has made it an appealing choice for college savings for some. However, recent changes to many companies' policies may limit the usefulness of this strategy. While a full analysis of this topic is beyond the scope of this book, it is something that should be reviewed with your advisor.

I felt it was important to mention this topic since saving and paying for college can often come at the expense of retirement savings and it is also an area where unfortunately, life insurance is sold with questionable merits. College planning is an area some insurance reps see as a target-rich environment. Let me explain:

It's back to school time, and if you're the parent of a high school student, you'll no doubt be invited to the financial aid presentation at the school. Innocent sounding enough - I'm sure you've got a lot questions about the financial aid process and having the opportunity to get some answers sounds like a great idea.

There's only one problem. If the presentation is given by anyone who isn't a counselor at the school, it's a very good chance it's a financial guy looking to strike. Here's how it usually goes: An outside *college planning advisor* gives a presentation that's designed to do nothing more than scaring the you-know-what out of you. They'll explain how important filling out the FAFSA correctly is and that errors could cost you thousands of dollars in financial aid. They'll probably liken it to a tax return and compare what errors there can cost you.

They'll also explain how moving money to certain financial products will shield it from the financial aid calculations and get your kids more aid. Sounds great - but wait for the sales pitch.

Their goal is to get you so scared that you'll agree to meet one-on-one with them to discuss your situation. For a nominal fee—usually starting around $1,500— they'll be happy to fill out your FAFSA and explain how they can reallocate your assets to maximize your financial aid and perhaps even save on taxes. That's sales speak for sell you a financial product. In the case of college planning, it's usually index universal life insurance.

The truth is that these so-called college planning advisors are nothing more than financial sales guys who seize on an annual opportunity to profit from your apprehension about a pretty important subject. As far as the financial gymnastics are concerned, yes, there are some things that may help you, but these are usually very simple and most likely won't provide the promised benefits. Any college financial planning that's going to really matter needs to be done when your kids are young, not at age 16, and should be part of your comprehensive financial plan. How else can you ensure that the college planning solution sold to you won't adversely affect other areas of your financial world? While the potential of a few additional dollars of financial aid may seem like a good thing today, the long-term cost, if understood, may not be so appealing.

Buy Term and Invest the Difference

If you've ever listened to the free-advice crowd, you may be convinced that cash value life insurance is an expensive waste of money. This has become the mantra of Suze Orman and Dave Ramsey. Instead, you should buy term insurance and invest the difference.

Forgetting for a moment that Suze's advice represents a bit of a conflict of interest, does this advice have merit? Surprisingly, in certain circumstances, it does.

When I use cash value life insurance in a financial plan, it is rarely for the death benefit. I use it for the other benefits I've discussed in this chapter. In fact, these policies are usually structured for maximum cash value, not death benefit. Using whole or universal life policies is a very expensive way to get a death benefit.

When a specific level of death benefit is needed, a combination of policies may be used where the bulk of the death benefit may come from term or guaranteed universal life (GUL), depending on the duration of the need. GUL is permanent universal insurance that can be structured with no cash build up, making it the least expensive form of permanent insurance.

The fact is that cash value life insurance is a really expensive way to get a death benefit. In the case of younger families who need large amounts of coverage, it is impractical to use cash value life. That doesn't stop the insurance guy from trying to sell it.

As far as always buying term and investing the difference, this advice, like much of the advice from the free advice crowd, uses bad math and questionable assumptions. Human nature and behavioral finance show that most people would never invest the difference, making the entire premise questionable.

Life insurance has many uses that go far beyond just a death benefit. You've now seen that there are many more assets available to execute your financial plan than just stocks and bonds. You owe it to yourself, your family, and your retirement dreams to fully understand and analyze all your choices, not just those that your guy wants to show you.

CHAPTER **14**

Tracking Your Progress and Staying on Course

What happens after your planning is complete and your plan is executed? The trip to and through retirement is a long journey. Your financial plan is supposed to be your roadmap to guide you on that journey. How can you tell if you're on track once you start heading down the road? Don't you think it might be a good idea to check your map occasionally to make sure you're heading in the right direction?

Periodic, at least annual, reviews with your advisor are the only way to ensure your retirement stays on track. Unfortunately, when it comes to reviewing performance, most individuals and advisors think this entails little more than a review of the financial instruments you own.

The Usual Portfolio and Product Review

Don't get me wrong, staying on top of your investments is vitally important. Unfortunately, the process that many advisors employ when doing periodic review meetings is pretty much a waste of time.

Most review meetings tend to follow the same script. I hear this story often. The advisor will present a stack of reports, the pretty chart, and graph type, which go into excruciating detail of the historical performance of your investments.

Chances are, the only thing you'll care about or understand is the annual return numbers. How'd you do last year? Is your balance larger than the previous year?

The conversation will focus on the market and their analysis (or most likely the analysis of an analyst at their company) of what transpired in the past year. Most people will understand just enough about these events to bobblehead along.

If you were lucky enough that your investments outperformed the market - however the advisor or his firm may define that - the advisor is probably running around the room exchanging high-fives with you and your spouse. He's a genius. If, on the other hand, the performance fell a bit short of expectations, he'd be explaining how volatility, the economy, politics, or aliens caused the shortfall in performance. It's just a short term blip. After all, you're in this for the long haul.

Regardless of your investment's performance, this meeting is all about face time. Your advisor's goal is to have you walk out of the meeting feeling pretty good about your situation. If successful, they've got you on the hook for another year.

This type of review does very little in helping you track your progress. It is, however, better than the annual reviews of the product jockeys whose goal it is to find out if there are any changes to your situation that would allow them to sell you more product. At this point, I don't think I need to elaborate on that point further.

Does simply looking at the annual performance of your investments matter when it comes to your retirement? If you outperform the market every year, does that ensure that your plan will come to fruition? Does beating the market ensure your financial success? Heck no. But, conversations about the market are what we have come to expect.

A Portfolio Review with Meaning

As I touched on in chapter 6, understanding the performance of your investments is a bit more involved than simply comparing year-end balances or how your performance stacked up against the S&P 500. Neither of these tactics has much value. If you are going to have a review of your investments - and you definitely should - let's do it in a way that will allow you to truly understand the performance of your investments and give you the information you need to make informed unemotional decisions.

The purpose of the investment review is to analyze, review, and understand the performance and characteristics of your investments so that actions, if necessary, can be taken. A comprehensive investment review should cover at least the following five metrics.

1. Portfolio performance versus an appropriate benchmark
2. Manager performance versus an appropriate peer group
3. The portfolio's *risk-adjusted* return
4. The portfolio's asset allocation
5. The performance of the portfolio versus the benchmark return of your financial plan

Let's take a look at each metric in some detail to understand what it means and how it will help you understand and manage your investment portfolio.

Portfolio performance versus an appropriate benchmark: Looking at portfolio returns by themselves can never give a true picture of performance. For this, you need to compare the performance of your portfolio against a suitable benchmark. The problem becomes finding an appropriate benchmark. That may not be as easy as it may appear. Most individual investors and many advisors simply compare all portfolios to a market index, such as the S&P 500. While this may be simple and easy, it's misleading and wrong.

A benchmark needs to be a representation of the portfolio you are comparing. Any index, regardless of how broadly based it may be, still only looks at a narrow segment of the market. Most individual investors hold a portfolio that is probably somewhat diversified, not only in stocks and bonds but also by geography and market capitalization. Comparing a diversified portfolio to an index such as the S&P 500 would be like comparing a Yugo to a Corvette. Yeah, they're both cars, but they're not all that comparable.

The most effective way to track the performance of a portfolio is to use not one index, but a benchmark that is composed of various indices. The composition of this blended benchmark should mirror the allocation of the assets in your portfolio. For example, for a portfolio invested 60 percent in a diversified stock portfolio and 40 percent in a diversified fixed income portfolio, the S&P 500 would be a poor benchmark as it only holds large capitalization stocks, which represents only one piece of the total portfolio. A more appropriate benchmark might be a blend of the *Dow Jones U.S. Total Market Index* and the *Barclays Capital U.S. Aggregate Bond Index.* If there were an international component, a suitable index would be added to the benchmark. The point here is that if you are going to track and compare your portfolio performance, make sure your comparison makes sense.

Even the most comparable benchmark will not be perfect. One reason is that the indices are simply a calculation based on the underlying securities. They do not include fees and costs associated with investing in a comparable portfolio, mutual fund, or other investment.

It is extremely hard to beat your portfolio's benchmark on a consistent basis—assuming it's a valid benchmark. While beating the benchmark should never be your goal, you do want to be close. The performance of your portfolio versus its benchmark will give you an indication of the abilities of the person managing your money or the validity of their model.

Investment returns, on a periodic basis, are often impacted by timing. Sometimes an investment manager will be a little early to the party when making a change to a portfolio. The timing of the trades may impact results in the short-term but benefit them in the long-term. You should never judge the performance of an investment manager based on short-term results. However, if poor performance persists, it might be time for a change.

Often, the use of specific benchmarks is a function of the reporting system in use by the advisor. For those advisors who have access to a wide array of investment managers, this should not be a concern. It's in their best interest (and yours) for them to understand the performance of each manager and if there needs to be a change. If, however, your advisor is trading his own portfolios or has a limited roster of managers, it will be up to you to understand the investment strategy and ascertain whether or not his performance measures and benchmarks are appropriate. This may not be an easy task.

Manager performance versus an appropriate peer group: All the investment managers, mutual funds, or other investments that reside in a particular category or sector are referred to as a Peer Group. Statistics are available that show how the performance of any investment manager or investment product stacks up against its peer group.

For example, let's say you're selecting an investment manager to manage a diversified portfolio of U.S. stocks. Knowing how each manager performs inside their peer group will be a tremendous help. You would obviously want an investment manager who is consistently at the top of his peer group as opposed to one who is at the bottom. You should always strive to select investment managers or investment products that are in the top quartile (top 25 percent) of their peer group.

As with benchmarking, short-term timing issues may affect where a manager ranks among his peers. Once again, decisions should never be made based on short-term results and never because of one bad period.

The portfolio's *risk-adjusted* return: One of the goals in creating a portfolio is to achieve the highest return possible while being exposed to the lowest amount of risk, for any given asset class. When comparing portfolios or simply reviewing your current investments, judging performance by simply looking at the annual rate of return doesn't tell the entire story. Risk-adjusted rate of return looks at the rate of return of a portfolio or any investment and adjusts it for the amount of risk that went into achieving that return.

For example, suppose two portfolios - Portfolio A & B - both returned eight percent for the previous year. While the return was the same, Portfolio B took significantly more risk to achieve the return. Which portfolio would be the better investment? Obviously, Portfolio A.

Now let's say that Portfolio B had an annual return of ten percent, still taking more risk. The decision is not as obvious now. Here, we need to compare the risk in each portfolio with the risk contained in the benchmark. Could it be that while Portfolio B is taking more risk than Portfolio A, it is actually in line with the benchmark? The lower performance of Portfolio A may, in this case, be caused by taking too little risk.

Calculating risk-adjusted returns is beyond the scope of this book. However, any competent advisor will understand and be able to explain the risk-adjusted return of your portfolio.

The risk in a portfolio will change over time for many reasons. Analysis of portfolio risk and risk-adjusted returns should be part of every review. A portfolio that was once appropriate for your purposes may no longer be so due to an increase or decrease in risk. What's the use of understanding your risk profile if you ignore it once your investments are in place? Combining changes in risk along with other metrics may give clues to potential problems lurking around the corner. Once again, first we manage risk.

The portfolio's asset allocation: As part of the financial planning process, together with your advisor, your asset allocation for your investments is established. Your asset allocation is the percentage of your investments in various asset classes. The allocation should be much more detailed than simply the percentage of stocks and bonds. That type of allocation has little value and is just lazy. Your allocation should be divided, not only by asset type, but further allocated by market capitalization (large cap, small cap, etc.), geography, or other factors. As discussed in chapter 12, your asset allocation will be based on your risk profile and the annual rate of return target you are attempting to achieve based on your goals.

The first question on asset allocation in a review meeting is whether the current asset allocation is still appropriate. Let's assume you're 15 years into your financial plan and retirement is fast approaching. Is the asset allocation from 15 years ago still appropriate given your current situation? Is the amount of risk the original allocation provided still desired as

Exhibit 14.1   Effects of Market Changes on Asset Allocation Percentages

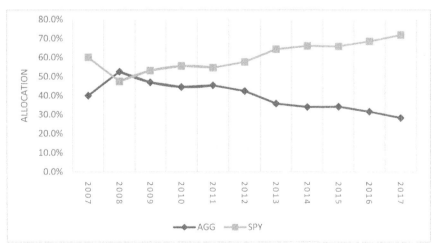

you enter retirement? Much has probably changed over that time, but often the asset allocation will remain unchanged.

Over time, the increase or decrease in the value of your investments will cause your asset allocation to change. Each year, your advisor should complete an analysis of the actual allocation of your assets versus the allocation that you established in the financial planning process.

This example shows the actual impact of a portfolio started January 1, 2008. The moderate risk portfolio consists of 60 percent S&P 500 ETF (ticker: SPY) and 40 percent US Aggregate Bond ETF (ticker: AGG.) Assuming the portfolio wasn't touched since then, the rise of the stock market since the beginning of 2009 has caused a large increase in the stock portion of the portfolio, throwing the asset allocation out of balance. The allocation to stocks is now greater than 70 percent, far greater than the target allocation. The portfolio can no longer be considered moderate. In many cases, the investor will be unaware that they are now taking more risk than originally intended.

The opposite issue may occur after a period of negative returns in the stock market. In this case, the change in asset values would cause the allocation of bonds to increase, perhaps reducing the risk and the expected rate of return of the portfolio below desired levels.

Changes in the asset allocation due to an increase or decrease in asset values must be corrected. We refer to this correction as *rebalancing* the portfolio. During rebalancing, assets are bought and sold to bring the portfolio back into balance with the desired asset allocation. Not only does this manage the desired risk in the portfolio, but it also reinforces the diversification benefits of the portfolio approach. In the case of appreciating assets, gains are locked in during the rebalancing process, lessening the effects of the inevitable market correction. In a down market, the opposite would occur, and stocks would be purchased at reduced prices in anticipation of the next market cycle. It's always better to buy on sale!

The performance of the portfolio versus the benchmark return of your financial plan: One component of the financial planning process is to set the target rate of return. This rate is the average return required, on an annual basis, to achieve the asset growth projected in your financial plan. Since the market doesn't return averages, your returns each year will most likely be higher or lower than the target rate.

While returns in any given year should not be a cause for concern, the persistent underperformance of your target, especially early in your plan or early in retirement, can cause shortfalls and will need to be addressed. Remember sequence-of-returns risk? Keep in mind, beating the market does not necessarily mean you are achieving your target.

Reviewing and managing your investments is imperative on your journey to and through retirement if you are to arrive at your desired destination. Hopefully, you can see that the process is far more involved than just looking at annual returns and account balances. Narrowly focused reviews of returns and balances accomplish nothing more than perpetuating the big number mentality and do little in the way of tracking your progress toward your retirement goals, as investment values are only one component of your financial plan.

Checking Your Map

Once your financial plan is complete, your asset allocation set, and your investments in place, the performance of your investments is pretty much out of your control. The skill of the investment manager and the mood of the market gods will determine your annual returns.

Now it's time to shift your focus. There's another lesson you must take away from this book: The financial markets are NOT the center of your financial universe. While the growth of your investments is certainly important, the market will not be what determines your success. The biggest driver of your financial success or failure is YOU. Stick to your plan and your odds of achieving your goals increases dramatically.

Your financial plan, properly constructed, considers your current financial condition, good or bad, and plans for the best outcome possible, given your resources. Past financial transgressions, such as excessive spending and debt, are included in your plan and cleaned up over time. Your completed plan contains your P&L and Balance Sheet, forecasting your cash flow, assets, and debt on a year-by-year basis.

Once your plan is in place, it's up to you to live up to the commitments you agreed to when you built your financial plan. The first step of the annual plan review process is to compare the forecast for the year with your actual performance. In short, did you live up to your commitment?

Financial planning is kind of like that New Year's resolution to lose weight and get back in shape. January 1st rolls around, and you're all gung-ho. You join a gym, buy some new gear, and start eating sprouts and kale. This time, you're going to do it!

By February 15th, you haven't been to the gym in a few weeks, your new gear is under the bed somewhere, and you find yourself sitting on the couch getting ugly with a bucket of KFC. The only exercise you get is going to the fridge for another beer. You get on the scale and see the bad news.

Many people are the same with their finances. You put together a financial plan and swear you'll stick to it. Things go fine for a while until your friends take an impromptu trip to Hawaii. Next thing you know, you and your spouse take an unplanned trip to Fiji. They buy an Audi; you buy a Mercedes - also not in your plan. My point is that the further you get away from the planning process, the less you remember why you did it in the first place. Retirement seemed like a priority at the time ... until other priorities took over.

Each year you must review your income, expenses, discretionary spending, and the additional amount you were supposed to save and invest. How do they compare to the forecast values from your plan? Did you live up to your commitment, or did you go off the rails?

Now, some things may be out of your control. A job loss will cause a reduction in income, and unplanned expenses can happen for many reasons. These, unfortunately, are a fact of life. Also, just like with your investments, timing may play a part. A large, planned expense made in December instead of January the following year, or, vice versa, will affect the current year values as compared to your forecast.

The main point here is that you must control the items that are in your control, such as discretionary spending. The periodic reviews of your financial plan are designed to hold you accountable. Think of it as climbing on the scale. The scale never lies.

Simply looking at your performance versus your plan, in any given year, only gives you a snapshot. It would be the same as only comparing your investments to their benchmark. Good information, but hardly actionable. Much more important is the trend over a period of years.

Each year, during the next part of the review process, the forecast values for the year are replaced with the actual values for income, expenses, spending, savings, etc., and a revised plan is created. Once completed, the revised plan is compared

Exhibit 14.2 Plan Trend Analysis

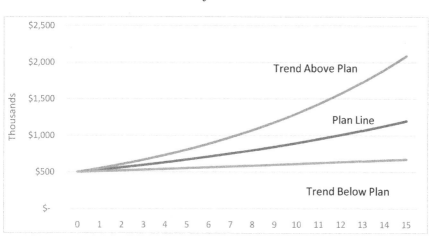

to the original plan. Over the course of three or four years, trends may begin to emerge. These trends may be positive or negative. Negative trends left unchecked can have unwanted effects on your retirement goals.

For example, let's assume you created your financial plan fifteen years before your anticipated retirement. During your annual review, five years into your plan, it becomes apparent that a negative trend is developing in your revised plan. What do you do?

First, you need to analyze the cause of the trend. Short-falls can occur for many reasons. Is it due to a few large, unplanned expenses, or is this trend a new reality that is going to continue? Can the trend be contained and corrected, or is there little you can do?

Once the cause of the trend is known, a solution can be developed. It's in situations such as this that your advisor earns his pay. You may be able to fix deviations with a few years of reduced spending.

Larger issues may require rethinking some of your retirement lifestyle expenses, or perhaps the problem can be solved by continuing to work for a few more years, if possible.

Whatever the solution, uncovering the negative trend ten years before retirement leaves plenty of time for corrective action. Having time to prepare is certainly better than finding out six months before you retire that you have a big problem. At that point, there may be very little that can be done.

Conversely, perhaps an unexpected promotion has led to a large unplanned increase in income at the same time your investments are enjoying a resurgent bull market. Your revised plan shows a nice positive trend. This sounds like an opportunity. What can you do?

In this case, I may look to lock in some of the market gains that are well above plan before they can evaporate in a market correction. One strategy for this may be to use the profits to generate additional guaranteed income into your retirement income plan. Could this unexpected windfall possibly allow you to retire a few years early? Wouldn't that be nice?

The journey to and through retirement can be long, and life seldom goes according to plan. Staying on course will take much more than simply checking the performance of your investments. Periodic reviews designed to uncover, analyze, and manage changes in your financial plan that occur over time allow you to correct problems and make midcourse adjustments to keep your plan on track. You can stop from time to time and check your map to make sure you're on course, or you can ignore it and hope you end up at the right destination. The choice is yours.

CHAPTER 15

It's Planning Time

Change is hard. It's even harder when you have no idea that you have a problem that requires change.

The emergence of the market-centric, do-it-yourself attitude and approach to investing, retirement planning, and personal finance in general didn't happen overnight. It was the product of the convergence of the growth of self-directed retirement plans and the explosion of free and easily obtained information and technology brought about by the dot-com boom and the Internet. It was an opportunity seized upon by the very people who benefit by it the most: the financial firms and their representatives, the gurus with something to sell, and the financial media that lives and breathes for viewership and ratings.

Through their well-orchestrated use of advertising and Jedi mind tricks, they created the myth that, regardless of how complicated your financial situation may be, the market is simple. You can solve any problem by simply using their tools and financial products to invest and plan for yourself. They have succeeded in diverting your attention away from your goals and on to theirs - to make money at your expense.

Now that you know the truth, I hope that, as you go forward, your focus will change. Instead of focusing on the day-to-day gyrations of the Dow, S&P, NASDAQ, gold, oil, or any other market indicator, your attention is now directed on you, your family, planning for your future, and achieving your goals.

The cautionary tale of Bob and Joan should serve as a warning - and a wake-up call. Your primary goal for your retirement is not your *big number*. It must be to ensure that you don't run out of money! You can only accomplish this through proper planning with a focus on the *small number* and using the financial products that are best suited to execute each piece of your plan.

Once again, **a financial product or portfolio is not your financial plan!** They are simply the tools you will use to make your plan work. I can't emphasize that point enough, but now you know better.

While I have covered quite a bit in this book, I've only scratched the surface. Depending on your unique situation, there will be other issues and concerns that will need to be addressed, such as estate planning, tax planning, charitable giving, Social Security planning, Medicare, and healthcare planning, just to name a few. This doesn't even consider special situations such as those faced by federal employees, medical professionals, and many other *special cases.* The product jockeys don't even know many of these issues exist.

Now that you understand the magnitude of the task at hand, is *your guy* - whomever that may be—really the best choice to help you and your family achieve your financial goals?

The good news is that with the knowledge you've gained in these pages, you should now understand more about the topics of planning and investing for retirement than most. In fact, you now probably know more than most of the sales guys who hide behind an advisor title.

Be aware that where you go from here is up to you. Success doesn't happen by accident. While there are those who will commit to taking the steps necessary to ensure their future, there are sadly those who will never get past the starting line. Every week, I hear from families that have the best intentions.

They want and need to plan for their future. Sadly, they never do - they are just too busy. The truth is, we're all busy. Most of us are just busy being busy. You can procrastinate, or you can act. It's time to turn this newfound knowledge into action.

What if...

The planning methodologies, strategies, and tactics that I've put forth in this book assume that the reader has both the time and assets to put them in place. What happens if you're reading this book and you haven't saved enough for retirement? Or, like many, you decided to begin the process of *thinking* about planning for retirement the day before - or day after - you retire? Is proper planning unavailable in these cases?

As I said previously, you can't change yesterday. The fact that your situation may not seem perfect doesn't change the fact that you need a financial plan and income strategy to help ensure you won't run out of money. Simply put, *sometimes you get to pick your goals, and sometimes your goals pick you!*

In the case of the family that thinks they didn't save enough for retirement, going through the planning process will enable them to see exactly what their situation is and how much income they can generate. The picture may not be as bleak as they think, as I often find families surprised at how much income their retirement savings can produce.

In the absolute worst case, where the income is insufficient to support the lifestyle the family would like, changes in retirement and lifestyle plans can be made. While the changes may be less than ideal or what was desired, often they can lead to a longer, happier retirement based on an understanding of their financial picture as opposed to the stress of the unknown and the risk of running out of money.

For the family that waited until the last minute to plan, the answer could be good or bad. Once again, completing a plan as soon as possible will give the family the financial answer as to what type of retirement lifestyle will be possible. When it comes to planning, time is one of your greatest assets.

It's never too late to start the planning process, regardless of your current situation.

Taking the Next Step

At this point, you may be feeling a bit overwhelmed. That's to be expected. It's not easy being asked to rethink just about everything you thought you understood about investing, the markets, the players, and planning for your future. At the same time, I hope you're feeling energized, excited, and eager to begin the process.

Finding an advisor to help you create and execute your retirement plan will not be an easy task. You may need to interview quite a few before you find the one who's right for your needs. They may not be easy to find. Don't rush and don't settle. As I have discussed, a good advisor can have a tremendous impact on your life, while choosing the wrong advisor can be a disaster.

To make your task a little easier, I summarized the main lessons in the book down to the following ten points. Commit them to memory or at least refer to them often. They are designed to keep you focused and on track:

1. Interview your guy (use questions in the appendix) to ensure they can help you achieve your goals and not just sell you something.
2. The key to financial success is to have a plan. It is your roadmap to your destination.
3. You must plan for the small number.
4. A product or portfolio IS NOT a financial plan.
5. Free or generic advice is dangerous and worth exactly what you pay for it.
6. You are not a trader.

7. First, you must manage risk. You must manage all risk, not just market risk.

8. Don't be a bobblehead! Fully understand everything before you commit your dollars.

9. Do not blindly believe what *you've heard,* what you're told, or what you read on the Internet.

10. Invest your money as the wealthy invest theirs.

When it comes to your financial future, be an active participant, never settle for less than what you need, and never compromise your goals.

My Invitation to You

As I was writing this book, I realized that just showing families how to plan for their future was not enough. I know how hard it is to find an advisor who can take care of all your financial needs. The truth is, while there are hundreds of thousands of people who use the advisor title, there are not that many who do the type of planning you need. Nothing could be worse than knowing you need help and not being able to find it.

Knowing how hard it would be to find the help you need, I decided to set aside time each month to work directly with the readers of this book. By getting to this point, you have demonstrated your desire for retirement success; the least I can do is help you get there.

If you are interested in applying to work with me directly, go to DontRunOutOfMoneyBook.com for details. Once you complete the short questionnaire, a member of my team will contact you. If you qualify, we could begin working on your plan for retirement success in just a few days.

Thank you for investing your time - and a few dollars - to read this book. I hope you found it enlightening, educational, and hopefully a bit entertaining. Your small investment should pay dividends in your life for years to come.

Since I entered this business, it has been my mission to get this message out to those who needed it most. If this book can prevent just one family from falling victim to the financial shenanigans of the sales guy or prevent another family from running out of money like Bob and Joan, it was well worth the time and effort it took for me to write.

Remember, you get only one shot at retirement. Let's make it count. Here's to your success!

David J. Seibel

Interviewing your Advisor

After reading this book, you should have a much better idea of the type of advisor you want and need to help you achieve your financial goals. During your initial consultation with an advisor, they will be asking you a series of questions to see if you are a good fit for their practice. You MUST find out if the advisor's practice is a good fit for you.

Listed below are a series of questions that will help you make that decision. Next to yourself, your advisor may be the person who will be most responsible for helping you achieve your financial goals. You must be sure they are the right person.

As I've said throughout the book, you must take an active role in your success. This is no time to be a bobblehead.

1. How are you licensed?

While an advisor may hold other licenses, there are three you should be concerned with:

- Investment Advisor (series 65/66)
- Registered Representative (series 6 or 7)
- Life (and possibly health) Insurance

This should always be the first question you ask since the answer could easily disqualify the advisor. If the advisor is only licensed and registered to sell securities or life insurance, their recommendations will only be based on those products. Your advisor must be able to work in both the investment and insurance markets to properly serve your needs.

2. Are you a fiduciary?

Unless the advisor is registered and acting in the capacity of an investment advisor, they are not a fiduciary. The now-defunct DOL rule and the early indications of an SEC rule specify a *best interest rule,* meaning the advisor must work in your best interest. While better than nothing, this is not a fiduciary relationship. Also, holders of the CFP designation will often refer to themselves as fiduciaries. They are not.

3. What financial experience do you have?

Does the advisor have extensive financial experience, or were they selling real estate or used cars before becoming an advisor?

4. Do you hold any advanced degrees or other credentials?

This is a bit of a trick question. Contrary to the propaganda, financial credentials, such as the CFP, ChFC, etc., should never be used to judge the competence of an advisor. Much of what is taught in these programs is academic and of limited value in the real world. Often, those who spend a lot of time talking about their credentials are the least qualified. Most good advisors who possess one of these credentials will rarely use them as a marketing tool. Beware of those who do. An advanced degree, specifically an MBA, may denote a higher level of financial knowledge as compared to others.

5. What services do you provide?

Make sure the advisor can provide ALL the services you need. These may include comprehensive financial planning, investments, insurance, estate planning, tax planning, or anything else you may need. Few advisors are experts in all these areas and will bring in experts where needed. Beware of the advisor who is an *expert* in every possible area. They are not.

6. Where are my assets held, and how safe are they?

Assets should be held in your account with a custodian such as Fidelity, Schwab, etc., and be a member of SIPC. They should never be held in the name of the advisor or their account. The advisor should have limited authority to move money only among accounts or to the account holder, never to a third party without prior authorization. Make sure you understand their answer.

7. How do you get paid?

A registered representative or insurance producer will get paid commission. An investment advisor will usually get paid a fee based on assets under management. If your advisor says they are fee-only, ask them how they get paid on insurance products. There is no good answer here. If they are insurance licensed, they are getting paid. Walk away.

8. What costs will I be subject to, and are these costs transparent?

It's one thing to understand how the advisor gets paid, but what about the other costs? Account fees, trading costs, expenses, etc., can add up. You should know what you are paying.

9. What is your client profile?

Most good advisors specialize in one area, such as retirement planning. Make sure the advisor you're talking with works with others who have your same issues.

10. What is your financial planning process?

See chapters 7 and 8. Is the process collaborative and detailed, or is the advisor using a black-box based on assumptions and rules-of-thumb? Ask for a copy of a financial plan to see if the result of the planning process meets your needs and expectations.

11. What is your investment process, and who is responsible for investment decisions?

See chapter 12

12. What is your client experience?

There is no right or wrong answer here. It relates to you getting the level of service that you require. How often do you want to see your advisor? What level of communication do you require? Each family may have different requirements. You want to ensure that your expectations are in alignment with the advisor's practice model.

I personally go over many of these topics in my first meeting with a prospective family. These questions, however, may be only the beginning. Your experiences may require clarification in other areas. Don't feel intimidated to question the advisor. Any good advisor will respect the questions you ask.

If the advisor is put off by your questions, that may be a sign that you need to look for another advisor.

Endnotes

1. Grinstein-Weiss, Michael. "How prepared are Americans for retirement: Written testimony to the Special Committee on Aging." Brooking Institute. March 12, 2 0 1 5 . https://www.brookings.edu/testimonies/how-prepared-are-americans-for-re-   tirement-written-testimony-to-the-special-commit- tee-on-aging/

2. McFarland, Brendan. "A Continuing Shift in Retirement Offerings in the Fortune 500." Willis Towers Watson. February 2018. https://www.towerswat- son.com/en-US/Insights/Newsletters/Americas/insider/2016/02/a-continuing-shift-in-retire-ment-offerings-in-the-fortune-500.

3. Williams, Terri. "The U.S. Ranks 14th In Financial Literacy." Investopedia. April 05, 2017. https://www.investopedia.com/articles/personal-finance/120115/us-ranks-14th-financial-literacy.asp.

4. *2017 RICP® Retirement Income Literacy Survey Report.* The American College of Financial Services. 2017. http://retirement.theamericancollege.edu/sites/retirement/files/2017_Retirement_Income_Literacy_Report.pdf

5. Landrum, Sarah. "Millennials, Technology and The Challenge of Financial Literacy" Forbes. August 4, 2017. https://www.forbes.com/sites/sarahlandrum/2017/08/04/millennials-tech-nology-and-the-challenge-of-financial-litera- cy/#6acldd0228e6

6. Lemoine, Craig W., and Ajamu Loving. *Financial Planning: Process and Environment.* Bryn Mawr, PA: American College Press, 2016. 2.

7. Ibid, 20.

8. Wang, Penelope. "You May Live Longer Than You Think. Here's How to Afford It." Time. March 15, 2016. http://time.com/money/collection-post/3481760/longevity-life-expectancy-lon- ger-gap/.

9. "Making Sense of Financial Professional Titles." Securities and Exchange Commission. https: / / www.sec.gov/files/ib_making_sense.pdf.

10. *Senior Designations for Financial Advisers.* Report. Consumer Financial Protection Bureau. April 18, 2013. https://files.consumerfinance.gov-/f/201304_CFPB_01derAmericans_Report.pdf.

11. "Share of Americans Investing in Stocks 2015 | Statistic." Statista. https://www.statista.com/ statistics/270034/percentage-of-us-adults-to-have-money-invested-in-the-stock-market/.

12. Jurkowitz, Mark, and Jesse Holcomb. "Return of CNN 'Crossfire' Injects More Opinion into Evening Cable News." Pew Research Center. September 09, 2013. http://www.pewresearch.org/ fact-tank/2013/09/09/return-of-cnn-crossfire- injects-more-opinion-into-evening-cable-news/.

13. Sorrentino, Mike. *Using Google to Discredit a Fear Monger.* Report. Sarasota, FL: Global Financial Private Capital. April 1, 2016.

14. Ibid

15. "U.S. Department of Labor Finalizes Fiduciary Definition and Conflict of Interest Rule." Proskau- er. April 19, 2016. https://www.proskauer.com/alert/us-department-of-labor-finalizes-fiducia-ry-definition-and-conflict-of-interest-rule

16. *DALBAR'S 20th Annual Quantitative Analysis of Investor Behavior 2014-Advisor Edition. Boston,* MA: DALBAR, 2014.5.

17. *DALBAR'S 23rd Annual Quantitative Analysis of Investor Behavior. Boston, MA: DALBAR, 2016. 5.*

18. Anderson, Tom. "Most Investors Didn't Come Close to Beating the S&P 500." CNBC. January 5, 2017. https://www.cnbc.com/2017/01/04/most-investors-didnt-come-close-to-beating-the- sp-500.html.

19. Bengen, William P. "Determining Withdrawal Rates Using Historical Data." *Journal of Financial Planning.* October 1994.

20. Ibid, 173.

21. Ibid, 179.

22. Ibid, 177

23. Bhojwani, Gary C. *Rethinking What's Ahead in Retirement.* Report. Allianz Life Insurance Company of North America. 15. April, 2011.

24. Zulz, Emily. "Morningstar's 'Must-Know' Stats About Long-Term Care." ThinkAdvisor. October 03, 2016. https://www.thinkadvisor.com/2016/10/03/morningstars-must-know-stats-about-long-term-care/?slreturn=20180512161135.

25. Emily Gurnon. "The Staggering Prices of LongTerm Care 2017." Forbes. September 26, 2017. https://www.forbes.com/sites/nextave-nue/2017/09/26/the-staggering-prices-of-long- term-care-2017/#42al97ef2ee2.

26. Ibid.

27. *2017 Investment Company Fact Book.* 57th ed. Investment Company Institute, 2017. 30.

28. Fan, Jack, and Marci Mitchell. "Equity-Bond Correlation: A Historical Perspective." *Graham Capital Management,* September 2017.

29. Miller, Mark. "Getting Something Back from LongTerm Care Insurance." *Wealth Management,* 46. April 20, 2016.

30. Ibid, 44.

31. Iacurci, Greg. "Life Insurance Helps with Retirement Planning but Beware of the Pitfalls." InvestmentNews - The Investing News Source for Financial Advisers. May 29, 2016. http://www.investmentnews.com/article/20160529/FREE/160529950/life-insurance-helps-with-re-tirement-planning-but-beware-of-the

About the Author

David J. Seibel is founder and Managing Partner of AGS Aurora Financial Services, LLC. Since the height of the financial crisis in 2008, Dave has been helping families manage their financial risk and develop plans for their financial future to help ensure they don't run out of money.

Dave has a Master of Science degree from Worcester Polytechnic University and a Master of Business Administration from Fordham University. Dave is also a Chartered Financial Consultant®.

Prior to beginning his entrepreneurial career in 2000, Dave held corporate finance and executive finance positions at companies such as Random House Publishing, Allied-Signal, Estee Lauder, Revlon, Coleman, where he was Treasurer, and Sunbeam, where he was Vice President, Chief Financial Officer, International.

Made in United States
North Haven, CT
18 June 2022

20316424R00150